CW01176450

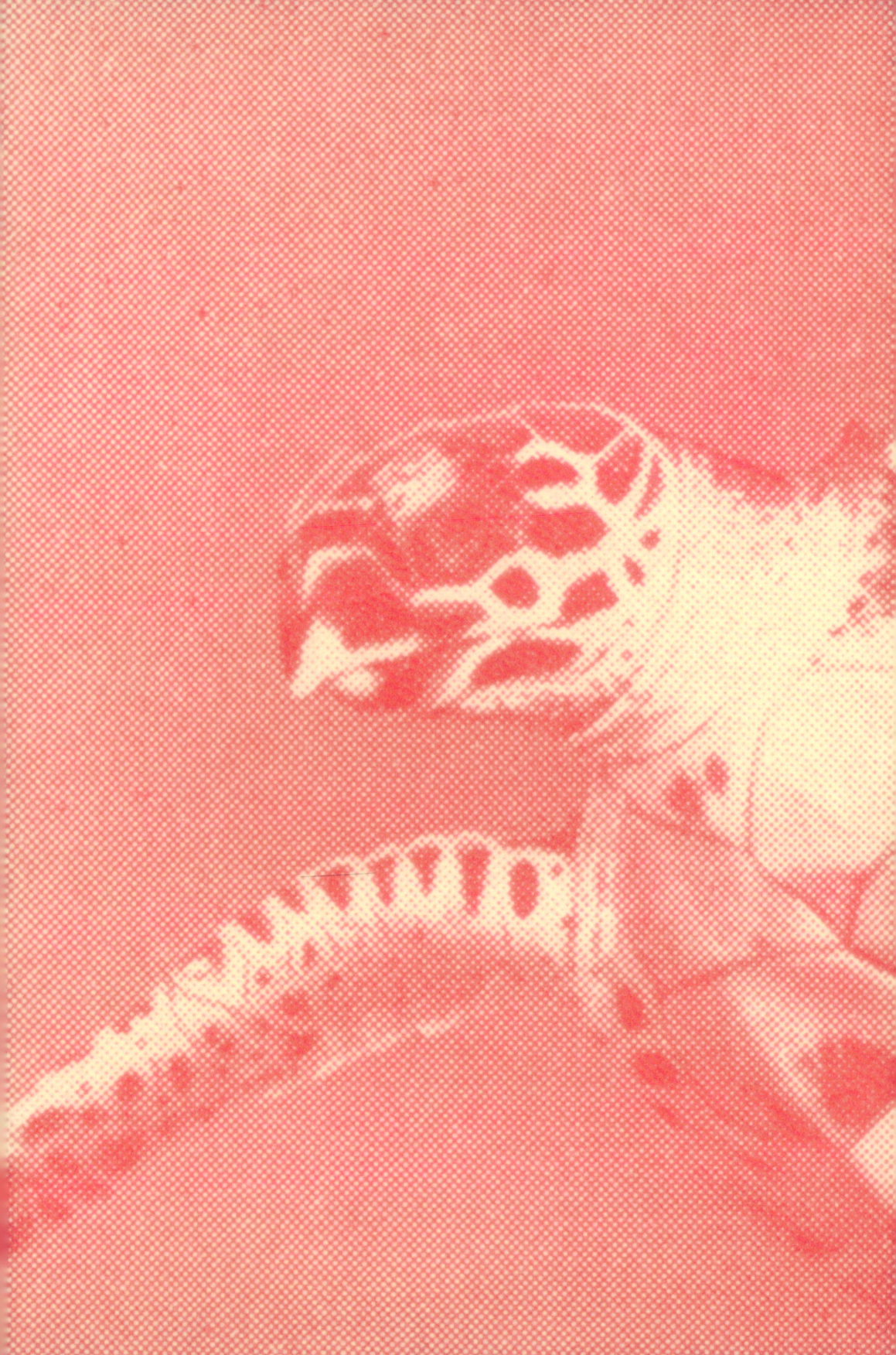

Die Plakatwelt ist beständig im Fluß. Für sie gelten d
Erscheinungen betrafen. Erscheinungen aber sind
tiert die Ereignisse. Sie ist ein Äußerstes an Welt. D
Augenblick, darauf beruht ihre Anziehung, aber auc
Modalitäten. Paul Eluard spricht von »boniment pha
den Ausdruck auf die Poesie. Bilder, Fotomontage
Objekte auf unsere Existenz; reale, mögliche, zufällig
und der Graphik, akustische und rhetorische Effek
ser Haut der Welt, unter der die Masken und Dekorati
Revolte gegen die Kunst aus der Tiefe, eine teleolo
einzufangen ist. Es gehört zu den untrüglichen Ken
Entscheidungen und Hoffnungen, ihren Lebensst
mindert die Gründe des Verschweigens und Verb
nicht versteckt. Die moderne Welt versammelt ih
chen. Geist ist eine Angelegenheit der Horizonte, nic
wertet, sie veräußert alles; ihre Montagen sind bede
Übertreibung, nur der Errichtung der künstliche
leuchtenden Plakate, die das jüngste körperliche un
die alten, verwaschenen Plakate, die ausverkaufte
sich jetzt erübrigt, denn sie werden niemanden me
sene Sphäre, ganz für sich, Opfer der Erinnerung, d
das gesellschaftliche Leben der Saison spiegelt d
vital und geistig wider, so daß es mehr und mehr
heiten kommt. [...] Wenn ein Plakat niemanden me
handhabt die Revision; sie muß sie handhaben, u
niemanden antrifft. Eine Plakatwelt hat ein tiefer

orte Heraklits, die nicht die Essenzen, sondern die
ignisse, *events*, sagt Whitehead. Die Plakatwelt poin-
uf beruht ihre Lebendigkeit. Sie legt fast zu viel in den
re Flüchtigkeit. Ihre Mittel sind gleichgültig wie ihre
stique«, von phantastischer Reklame, und bezieht
exte, fundamentalontologische Projektionen aller
reale Konfigurationen, optische Effekte der Malerei
es Hörspiels und der Revue, sie alle arbeiten an die-
en unnütz werden. Die Plakatwelt ist eine artistische
he Vitalität der Fläche, die, einmal befreit, nicht mehr
ichen der modernen Welt, daß sie ihre wesentlichen
nd ihre Geistesverfassung nach außen drängt. Sie ver-
ns. Sie ist zweideutig, aber diese Zweideutigkeit wird
ichtigen Objekte und Erfahrungen auf den Oberflä-
er Tiefe. […] Die moderne Welt ist komplex. Sie ver-
nlos und unbeschränkt, wenn sie, artistisch bis zur
mwelt dienen. […] In jeder Saison gibt es die weithin
istige Make up präsentieren, aber unter ihnen liegen
ler schlecht gewordenen Waren, deren Präsentation
treffen, aber sie bilden dennoch eine abgeschlos-
ständig die neuen Gewohnheiten heimsucht. Und
chichten der Plakatwelt, eine Folge von Oberflächen,
ner totalen Gegenwart der diskordanten Vergangen-
trifft, hat es seinen Sinn verloren. Jede Plakatwelt
e Gefahr der leeren Welt zu vermeiden, in der man
edürfnis nach Kommunikation als jede andere Welt.

Max Bense: Plakatwelt [1952]

Br

The poster world is always in flux. Here the words
rather appearances. Yet appearances are Ereigniss
emphasizes these events. It is an utmost concentra
almost too much in the moment, upon which its attra
indifferent as its modalities. Paul Eluard speaks
employing the term in a poetic sense. Pictures, pho
of all objects upon our existence; real, possible, coin
ing and graphics, acoustic and rhetorical effects of th
world skin, beneath which masks and decoratio
against art originating from depth. It is, rather, a te
never be recaptured. One of the inevitable disting
externalizes its most significant decisions and hope
ing of silence and concealment. It is ambiguous, bu
its important objects and experiences on its surface
modern world is complex. It exploits everything, alie
boundless when they, artistic to a fault, only serve
brings brightly illuminated posters presenting th
them lie the old, faded posters displaying the sold-o
as they will not engage anyone. They nevertheless co
of memory that constantly haunts the latest fashion
world's layers, a series of surfaces, each vital and stim
discordant pasts. [...] If a poster no longer engages a
revision: it has to in order to avoid the danger of a
world has a deeper need for communication than a

eraclitus apply—not those regarding essence, but
ents, according to Whitehead. The poster world
 of world, upon which its liveliness is based. It puts
on is based, but also its volatility. Its means are as
oniment phantastique", of fantastic advertisement,
ontages, texts, fundamentally ontological projections
ental, unreal configurations, optical effects of paint-
dio play and the revue; they all function upon this
come useless. The poster world is an artistic revolt
ogical vitality of the surface, which, once freed, can
ing features of the modern world is that it forcibly
 lifestyle and state of mind. It diminishes the reason-
is ambiguity is not hidden. The modern world collects
tellect is a matter of horizons, not depths. [...] The
es everything; its montages are unscrupulous and
tablish the artificial environment. [...] Each season
test physical and intellectual makeup, but beneath
inferior goods whose presentation is now pointless,
itute a closed sphere, a world unto itself, a victim
d the social life of the season reflects the poster
ting anew, becoming more and more a total present of
e, it loses its meaning. Each poster world utilizes
npty world where there is no one to encounter. A poster
her world. The surfaces are colder than the depths [...]

Max Bense: Plakatwelt [1952]

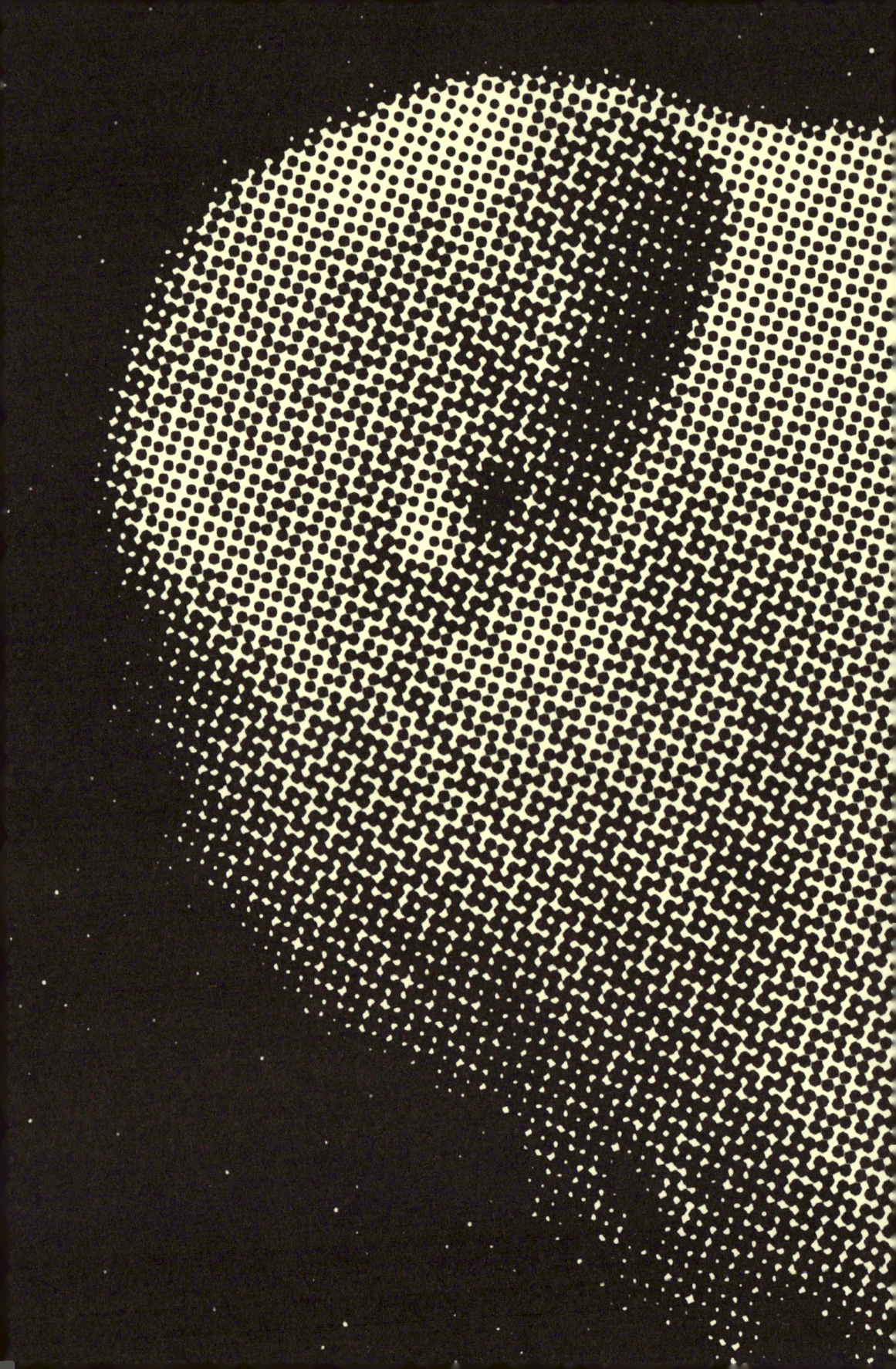

Das Plakat, so erläutert Cassandre, muß von Leuten gesehen werden, die sich nicht bemühen, es zu sehen. Die Plakatwelt ist von äußerster Helle, aber die Dinge werden ja nicht nur in der Finsternis unsichtbar, sondern auch im grellen Licht, und es bedarf demnach innerhalb der Warensphäre, in der das Sein darin besteht, daß man sie anpreist, einer erhöhten Intensität der Gegenstände, um als Ware, das heißt als Zugehöriges zur neuen Welt erkannt zu werden. Das Make up der Wesen und Ereignisse, von Hollywood bis Rom, vom Filmgesicht bis zur Marienerscheinung, die dann dementiert wird, weil die Erleuchtung nicht ausreichte, ist das erste und die Provokation das letzte Mittel der teleologischen Intention. Die Folge ist, daß schließlich auch unsere Intelligenz, also der Gedanke und das Wort, die Komposition und der Kalkül, Ideen und Metaphern, Epik, Prosa und Poesie, sich der intensionalen Formen bedienen müssen, um innerhalb der technologischen und provokatorischen Plakatwelt von den Leuten gesehen zu werden, die sich nicht bemühen, sie zu sehen. Und natürlich ist es ein Irrtum zu glauben, die Plakatwelt besäße keine Tiefe, sei flach, zweidimensional. Wie die Ware ihre echten Hintergründe hat, ein »sehr vertracktes Ding ... voll metaphysischer Spitzfindigkeit« sagt Marx, so kann man

Max Bense: Plakatwelt [1952]

The poster, as Cassandre explains, must be seen by people making no effort to see it. The poster world is one of extreme brightness. But things are invisible not only in darkness, but also in glaring light. Therefore, within the sphere of goods, where being inside the sphere means advertising it, there needs to be an elevated intensity of objects in order to achieve their recognition as goods, that is, as things belonging to the new world. The makeup of objects and events from Hollywood to Rome, from the actor's face to an apparition of the Virgin Mary, which is then denied because of inadequate illumination, is the first—and provocation the last—means of teleological intention. The result is that, finally, even our intelligence—that is to say thought and word, composition and calculation, ideas and metaphors, epic, prose and poetry—all have to make use of intensional forms within the technological and provocative poster world in order to be seen by people making no effort to see them. And, of course, it is a mistake to believe the poster world possesses no depth, is flat, two-dimensional. Just as products have their true backgrounds (a "very tricky thing ... full of metaphysical sophistry", according to Marx), one can peel off the layers of the poster world individually, freeing sections of modalities, penetrating the outer, cold

Max Bense: Plakatwelt [1952]

POSTERS/PLAKATE
1997–2017

Günter Karl Bose

for musica viva
für musica viva

POSTERS / PLAKATE
1997–2017

2017

Vorwort

Die Münchner *musica viva*-Konzertreihe widmet sich der Musik der Moderne und Avantgarde, insbesondere aber der Förderung und Aufführung der Musik, die heute von Komponisten geschaffen wird. Zahllose Werke wurden von der *musica viva* in den über 70 Jahren ihres bisherigen Bestehens in Auftrag gegeben und in ihren Veranstaltungen uraufgeführt.

1945 wurde die Konzertreihe von dem in München lebenden Komponisten Karl Amadeus Hartmann ins Leben gerufen. 1948 wurde sie dem gerade gegründeten Bayerischen Rundfunk integriert. Mit dem 1949 von dem Dirigenten Eugen Jochum gegründeten Symphonieorchester des Bayerischen Rundfunks steht der *musica viva*-Konzertreihe seither ein Orchester von internationaler Weltgeltung als fester Partner zur Seite, das sich in mehreren über die Saison verteilten Veranstaltungen, zusammen mit dem Chor des Bayerischen Rundfunks, mit Komponisten, Dirigenten, Solisten und weiteren Gastensembles, den Herausforderungen der Gegenwartsmusik stellt.

Die Konzerte gehören zu den zentralen Ereignissen des Kulturlebens der Stadt München, die internationale Beachtung finden. Sie werden vom Bayerischen Rundfunk nicht nur veranstaltet, sondern auch mitgeschnitten, produziert, in kommentierten Sendungen über Bayern hinaus und bisweilen europaweit übertragen. »The importance of *musica viva* in the cultural life of 800-year-old Munich is known to the whole world«, notierte Igor Strawinsky 1958.

Der leitende Gedanke, dass Musik vor allem eine Sprache der Gegenwart ist und dass es darauf ankommt, ein Forum zu etablieren, in dem eben diese, von Komponisten geschaffene Gegenwart zur Aufführung kommt, hat den Gründervater Karl Amadeus Hartmann von Anfang an auch besonderen Wert auf die Gestaltung der mit der *musica viva*-Konzertreihe verbundenen Plakate und Publikationen legen lassen. Bedeutende Grafiker und bildende Künstler gewann er hierfür: von Helmut Jürgens und Walter Tafelmeier bis zu Jean Cocteau, Le Corbusier und Emilio Vedova.

1997 übernahm Günter Karl Bose die visuelle Gestaltung der Plakate und Publikationen der *musica viva*-Konzertreihe des Bayerischen Rundfunks. In den vergangenen 20 Jahren entstanden für die *musica viva*, neben zahllosen Programmbroschüren, Büchern, Postkarten, CD-Booklets und Zeitungen, aus seiner Hand 164 Plakate zu rund 300 Veranstaltungen. Die Plakate sind seit langem schon zu begehrten Sammlerobjekten geworden. Nichts als überfällig ist demnach eine Publikation, die diese über einen langen Zeitraum entstandene Plakatwelt gleichsam auf einen Blick erlebbar werden lässt.

Entstanden ist eine Bildsprache, die der *musica viva* in der von Visualität bestimmten Öffentlichkeit ein einzigartiges und unverwechselbares »Gesicht« gegeben hat. Alles unterliegt in dieser Bildsprache dem steten Wandel und der permanenten Neuerfindung. Darin zeigt sie sich ganz dem Gedanken der Gegenwart verpflichtet und darin gleicht sie zutiefst der musikalischen Programmarbeit der *musica viva*-Konzertreihe.

Boses Plakate haben sich als Werbeinstrumente erster Güte erwiesen. Zugleich aber sind sie viel mehr als das. Sie preisen die Musik nicht als ein Produkt oder eine Ware an, die käuflich zu erwerben wäre. Sondern seine Plakate sprechen mit den Mitteln der Kunst eine Einladung aus: am Erlebnis der Kunst, der Konzerte und der präsentierten Werke teilzunehmen. Als deren Ankündigungen sind sie selbst zu Ereignissen sui generis geworden: Ereignisse für die Augen, die Ereignisse für die Ohren ankündigen. Man könnte von den Plakaten durchaus als visuellen Konzerten sprechen. Freilich wird strategisch den Augen nicht verraten, was für die Ohren zu erleben bestimmt ist. Die Plakate von Günter Karl Bose inszenieren die Überraschung; sie verraten nichts. Darin gleichen sie guten Buchtiteln, von den Theodor W. Adorno einmal sagte, sie seien so nahe an den in den Büchern zum Austrag kommenden Sachen, dass sie deren Verborgenheit achteten.

Winrich Hopp
Künstlerischer Leiter der *musica viva* des Bayerischen Rundfunks

Foreword

Munich's *musica viva* concert series is dedicated to modern and avant-garde music with special emphasis on the promotion and performance of music created by today's composers. Over the 70 years of its existence, *musica viva* has both commissioned and premiered countless works.

The concert series was brought into being in 1945 by Munich composer Karl Amadeus Hartmann. In 1948, it was incorporated into the newly founded Bayerischer Rundfunk (Bavarian Broadcasting). Since the Symphonieorchester des Bayerischen Rundfunks (Bavarian Radio Symphony Orchestra) was established by conductor Eugen Jochum in 1949, *musica viva* has enjoyed the steadfast partnership of an orchestra of international standing. Together, they face the challenges of contemporary music in several performances over the course of the season in collaboration with the Chor des Bayerischen Rundfunks (Bavarian Broadcasting Choir), composers, conductors, soloists and guest ensembles.

The *musica viva* concerts are among the main events of Munich's cultural life and receive international recognition. They are not only presented by Bayerischer Rundfunk, but also recorded, produced and transmitted by the broadcaster all across the state of Bavaria (and sometimes throughout Europe) as hosted radio programs. "The importance of *musica viva* in the cultural life of 800-year-old Munich is known to the whole world", as Igor Stravinsky wrote in 1958.

For Karl Amadeus Hartmann, the guiding principle was that music is above all a language of the present, and he knew the value of establishing a forum in which precisely this present, the product of composers' creative efforts, could reach the stage. From the very beginning, this principle led the founding father of *musica viva* to place great significance on the composition of the posters and publications that would represent it. For the task, he recruited a range of important visual and graphic artists: from Helmut Jürgens and Walter Tafelmeier to Jean Cocteau, Le Corbusier and Emilio Vedova.

Günter Karl Bose took over the composition of the posters and publications for Bayerischer Rundfunk's *musica viva* in 1997. Over the past 20 years, he has produced 164 posters for roughly 300 performances in addition to countless program brochures, postcards, CD booklets and newspapers. The posters have long been sought-after collector's items, making a publication that allows the complete evolution of this poster world to be experienced simultaneously in a single volume nothing less than overdue.

What Bose has rendered is a pictorial language that gives *musica viva* a unique and unmistakable "face" in the visually defined public sphere. In this language, nothing is more essential than constant change and a permanent state of reinvention. Here it becomes evident how completely committed Bose's pictorial language is to the present, a quality his work reflects with great resonance as it is intrinsic to the programming of the *musica viva* concert series.

Bose's posters have proven to be exceptional promotional instruments, yet they are much more than that. They praise music not as a product or ware that might be obtained through purchase. Art is employed as a means to express an invitation to participate in the experience of art, the concerts, the works presented. In announcing events, the posters become sui generis events themselves: events for the eyes proclaiming events for the ears. Though one might even describe them as visual concerts, strategically, of course, what is meant for the ears to experience is not divulged to the eyes. Karl Günter Bose's posters stage surprise; they betray nothing. In this way, they resemble good book titles in the sense that Theodor W. Adorno once expressed when he said that a good title is so close to the matters treated within its book that it respects their secrecy.

Winrich Hopp
Artistic Director
Bayerischer Rundfunk's *musica viva*

1997.98
offset print
CMYK

1997.98 01
Konzert > 24. Oktober 1997
Birkenkötter, Hidalgo,
Neuwirth, Hartmann
A0 [1189 x 841 mm]

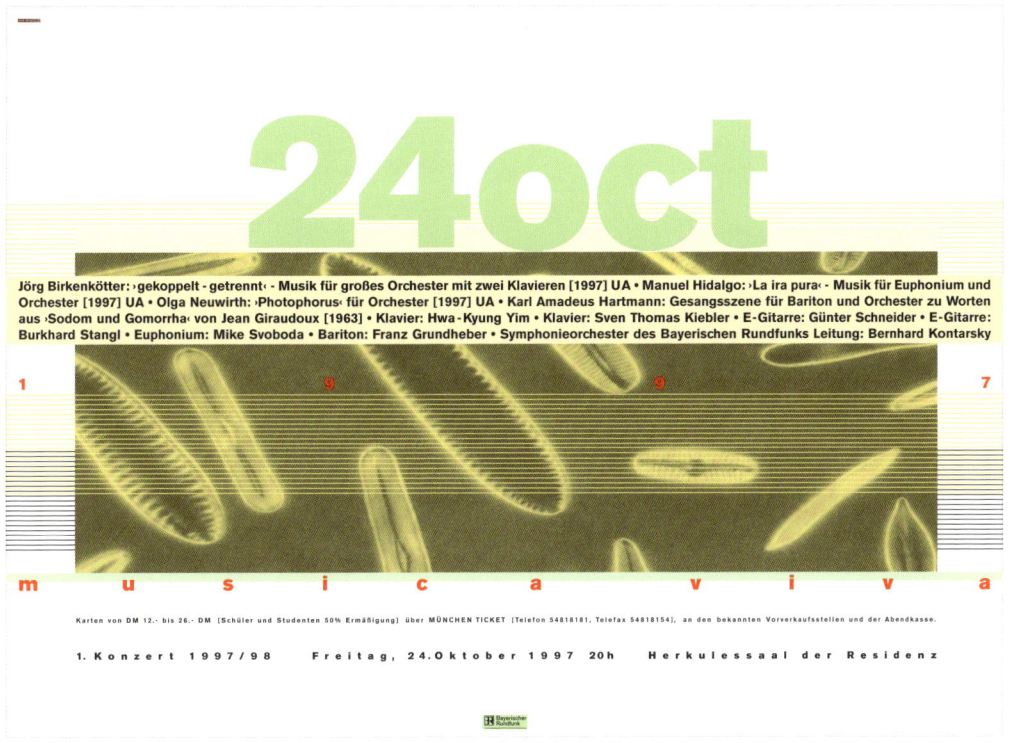

1997.98 02
Konzert > 14. November 1997
Messiaen, Szymanski, Varèse
A0 [1189 x 841 mm]

1997.98 03
Konzert > 12. Dezember 1997
Newman, Cowell, Volans, Xenakis
A0 [1189 x 841 mm]

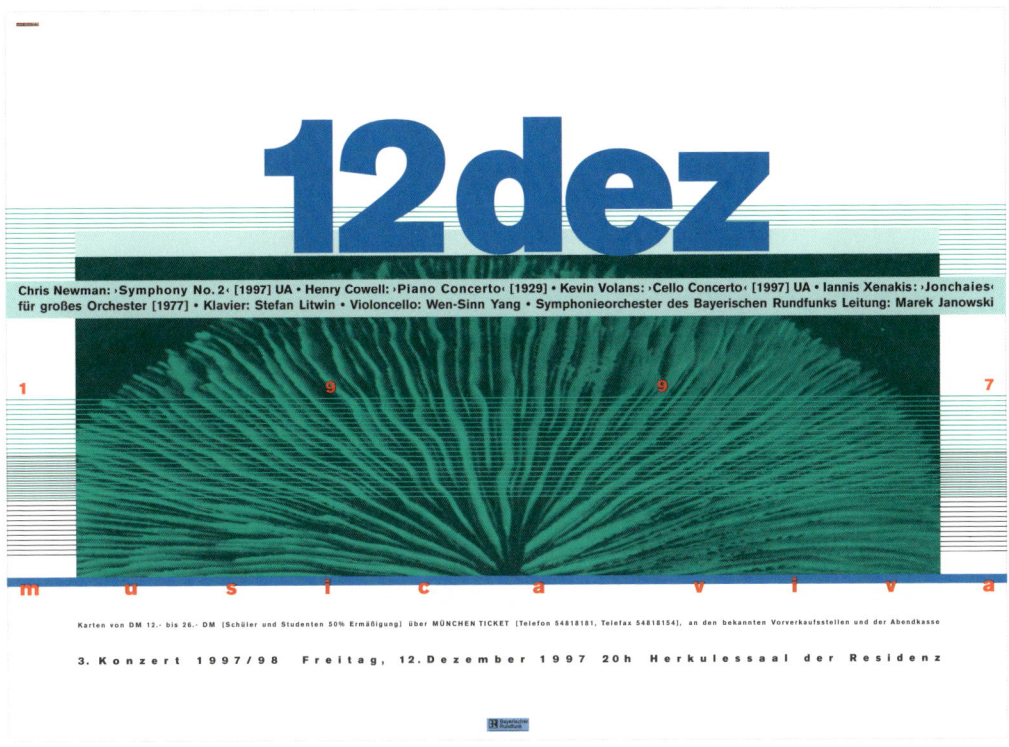

1997.98 05
Konzerte > 4./5. April 1998
PLAYER PIANO FESTIVAL
Barlow, Baynov, Heisig, Johnson,
Ligeti, Nancarrow
A0 [1189 x 841 mm]

1997.98 07
Konzert > 25. Juni 1998
50 JAHRE MUSIQUE CONCRÈTE
Gruppe Recherches Musicales
Bayle, Lejeune, Parmegiani, Schaeffer,
Teruggi, Zanési
A0 [1189 x 841 mm]

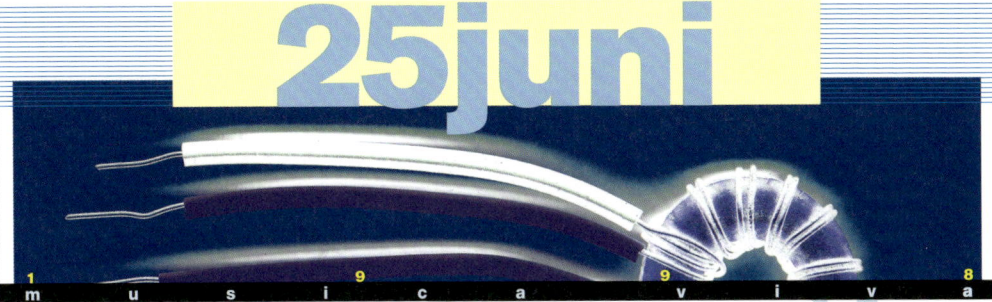

1998.99
offset print
CMYK

1998.99 02
Konzert > 16. Oktober 1998
Koch, Mello, Lutosławski
A0 [1189 x 841 mm]

1998.99 06
Konzert > 7. Mai 1999
MIKROINTERVALLE
Heyn, Hilario, Scelsi,
Wyschnegradsky, Xenakis
A0 [1189 x 841 mm]

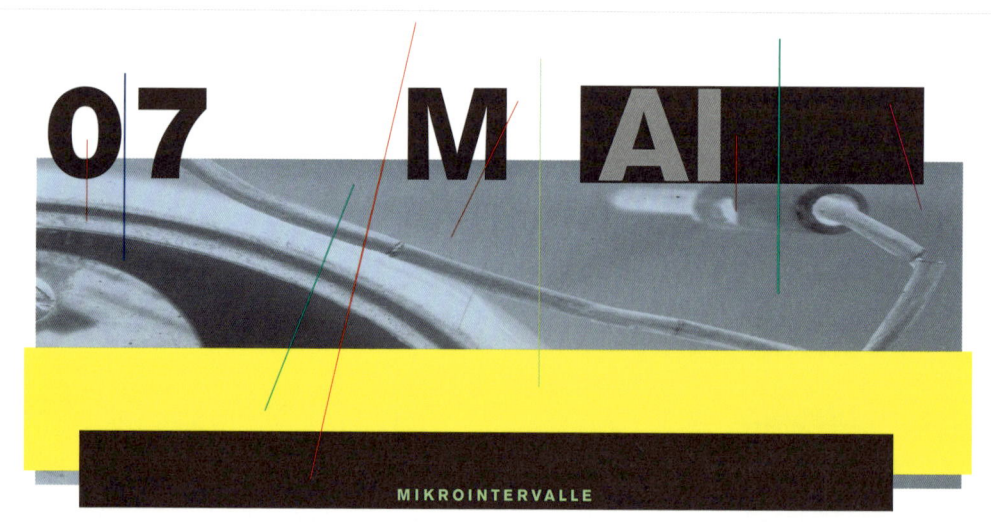

1998.99 07
Konzert > 24. Juni 1999
MUSIK FÜR NEUE INSTRUMENTE
Schläger, Stache, Staub, Tenney, Trimpin
A0 [1189 x 841 mm]

1999.00
offset print
CMYK

1999.00 01
Konzert > 8. Oktober 1999
Colla, Manav, Boulez
A0 [841 x 1189 mm]

1999.00 02
Konzert > 12. November 1999
Fritsch, Rihm, Ives
A0 [841 x 1189 mm]

1999.00 03
Konzert > 17. Dezember 1999
Berio
A0 [841 x 1189 mm]

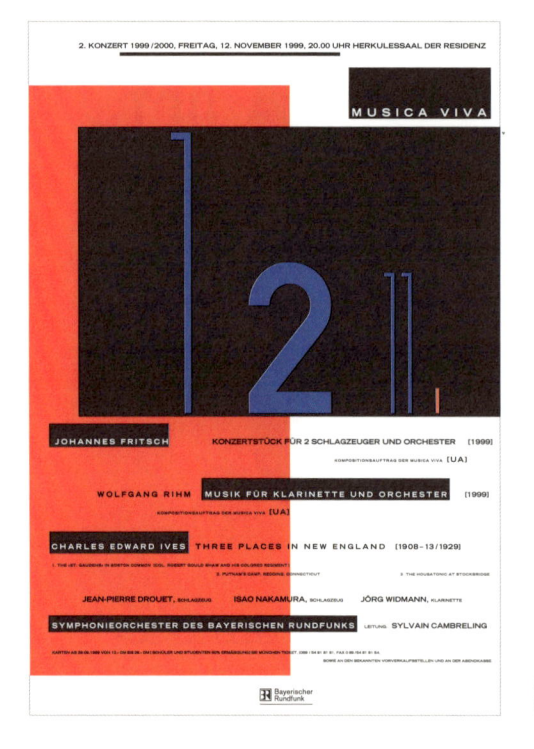

BE
17.

1999.00 06
Konzert > 16. Mai 2000
Riessler
A0 [841 x 1189 mm]

1999.00 08
Konzert > 8. Juni 2000
Zappa
A0 [841 x 1189 mm]

2000.01
offset print
CMYK + Gold / Pantone 804

2000.01 06
Konzerte > 26. / 27. April 2001
LAUTPOESIE /–MUSIK
A0 [841 x 1189 mm]

2000.01 07
Konzert > 4. Mai 2001
Hosokawa
A0 [841 x 1189 mm]

040501
040501
040501
040501
040501
040501
040501
040501

0 4 0 5 0 1
HERKULESSAAL DER RESIDENZ
VIERTES KONZERT DER MUSICA VIVA 2000/2001
FREITAG/4. MAI 2001/20 UHR/
MUSICA VIVA PREIS DER ARD UND BMW AG/
PREISTRAEGERKONZERT/
DER MILLENNIUMSAUSSCHREIBUNG/2000/2001/
DES BMW KOMPOSITIONSPREISES/
DER MUSICA VIVA/
TOSHIO HOSOKAWA/VOICELESS VOICE
IN HIROSHIMA [2000/2001]/URAUFFÜHRUNG/
FUER SOLISTEN SPRECHER/CHOR
UND GROSSES ORCHESTER/
NATHALIE STUTZMANN/ALT/
AUGUST ZIRNER/SPRECHER/
CHOR UND SYMPHONIEORCHESTER/
DES BAYERISCHEN RUNDFUNKS/
LEITUNG/SYLVAIN CAMBRELING/

040501
040501

2000.01 08
Konzerte > 17. / 18. Mai 2001
KOMPONISTEN IM IRCAM
INSTITUT DE RECHERCHE ET
COORDINATION ACOUSTIQUE / MUSIQUE
A0 [841 x 1189 mm]

2001.02
offset print
CMYK

2001.02 05
Konzert > 26. April 2002
Risset, Goeyvaerts,
Hölszky, Turnage
A0 [841 x 1189 mm]

2001.02 04
Konzert > 11. April 2002
Xenakis, Feiler, Zeller, Vierk, Goeyvaerts
A0 [841 x 1189 mm]

2001.02 06
Konzert > 7. Mai 2002
Kagel
A0 [841 x 1189 mm]

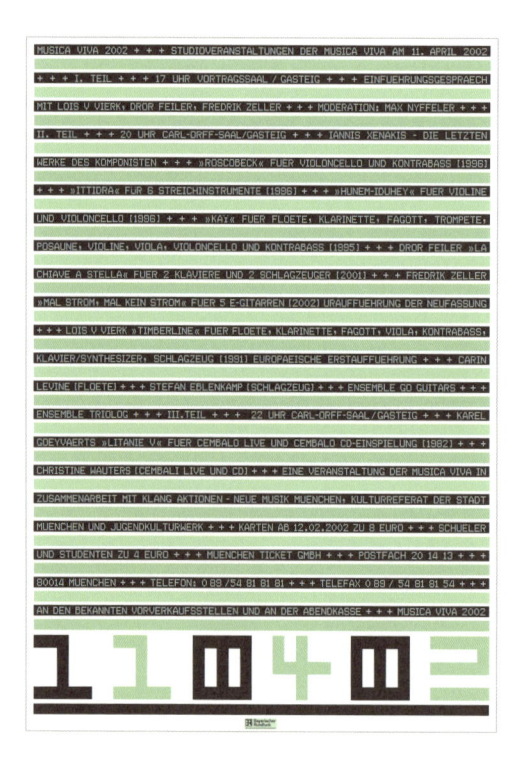

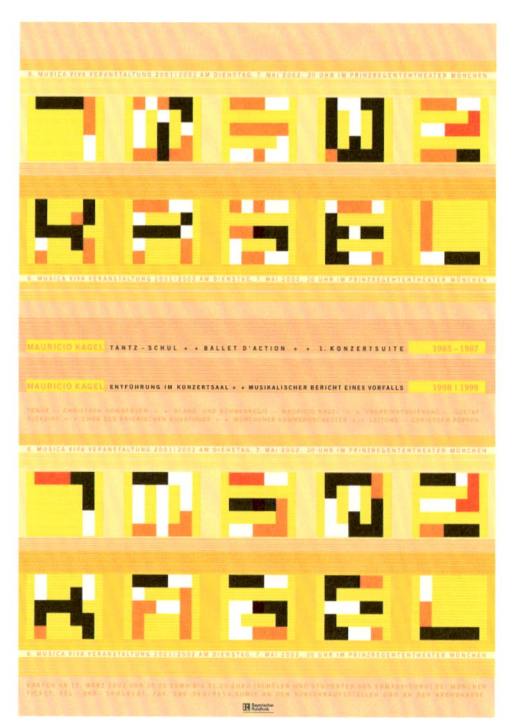

2001.02 07
Konzerte > 7. Juni 2002
Ligeti, Dillon, Wolff, ter Schiphorst,
Wolpe, Feldman
A0 [841 x 1189 mm]

7. VERANSTALTUNG DER MUSICA VIVA 2001/2002
// AM FREITAG, 07. JUNI 2002 //

1. TEIL: 17 UHR // BLACK BOX / GASTEIG
EINFUEHRUNGSGESPRAECH MIT DEN KOMPONISTEN UND INTERPRETEN /
MODERATION: FRIDEMANN LEIPOLD //

2. TEIL: 20 UHR // CARL-ORFF-SAAL / GASTEIG
GYOERGY LIGETI: "SIPPAL, DOBBAL, NADIHEGEDUEVEL" FUER MEZZOSOPRAN UND
4 SCHLAGZEUGER (2000) //
JAMES DILLON: "STUDIES" FUER AKKORDEON (2001) URAUFFUEHRUNG //
CHRISTIAN WOLFF: "SHE HAD SOME HORSES" FUER ALTZITHER, VIOLA (2001) URAUFFUEHRUNG
/ "BALANCING" FUER AKKORDEON (2002) URAUFFUEHRUNG //
IRIS TER SCHIPHORST: "MY SWEET LATIN LOVER" FUER VERSTAERKTE FLOETE, SAMPLE-
KEYBOARD, 2 PERCUSSIONISTEN UND E-GITARREN QUINTETT (2001/2002) URAUFFUEHRUNG //

AKKORDEON: TEODORO ANZELLOTTI / MEZZOSOPRAN: KATALIN KAROLYI / FLOETE: SARAH HORNSBY
/ VIOLA: KELVIN HAWTHORNE / ZITHER: GEORG GLASL / KEYBOARD: THOMAS HELL //
GOGUITARS, PERCUSSION ART QUARTET

3. TEIL: 22 UHR // CARL-ORFF-SAAL / GASTEIG
STEFAN WOLPE ZUM 100. GEBURTSTAG
STEFAN WOLPE: "ENACTMENTS FOR THREE PIANOS" (1950/1953)
MORTON FELDMAN: "TWO PIECES FOR THREE PIANOS" (1965/1966)
STEFAN WOLPE: "ENACTMENTS FOR THREE PIANOS" (1950/1953)
KLAVIERE: JOSEF CHRISTOF, IRMELA ROELCKE, BENJAMIN KOBLER // DIRIGENT: JAMES AVERY

Bayerischer Rundfunk

EINE VERANSTALTUNG DER MUSICA VIVA IN ZUSAMMENARBEIT MIT KLANG AKTIONEN - NEUE MUSIK MUENCHEN,
KULTURREFERAT DER STADT MUENCHEN UND JUGENDKULTURWERK.
KARTEN AB 9.4.2002 ZU 8.- EURO, SCHUELER UND STUDENTEN ZU 4.- EURO,
BEI MUENCHEN TICKET GMBH, POSTFACH 20 14 13, 80014 MUENCHEN, TEL.: 089 / 54 81 81 81, FAX 089 / 54 81 81 54,
SOWIE AN DEN BEKANNTEN VORVERKAUFSSTELLEN UND AN DER ABENDKASSE.

2002.03
offset print
CMYK

2002.03 01
Konzert > 11. Oktober 2002
Cage
A0 [841 x 1189 mm]

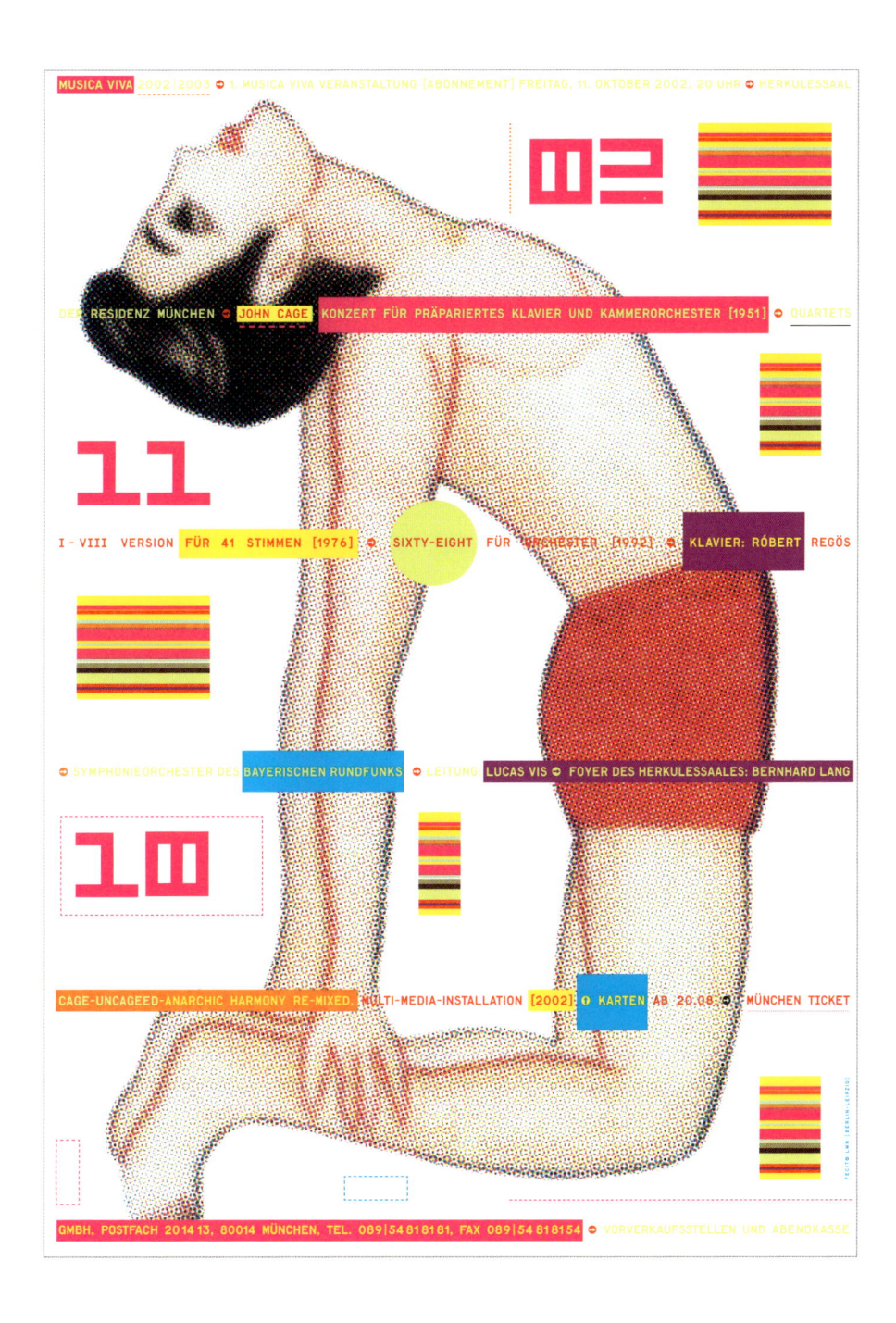

2002.03 02
Konzert > 15. November 2002
Wolpe, Richter de Vroe, Feldman
A0 [841 x 1189 mm]

2002.03 03
Konzert > 17. Januar 2003
Hillborg, Raskatov, López
A0 [841 x 1189 mm]

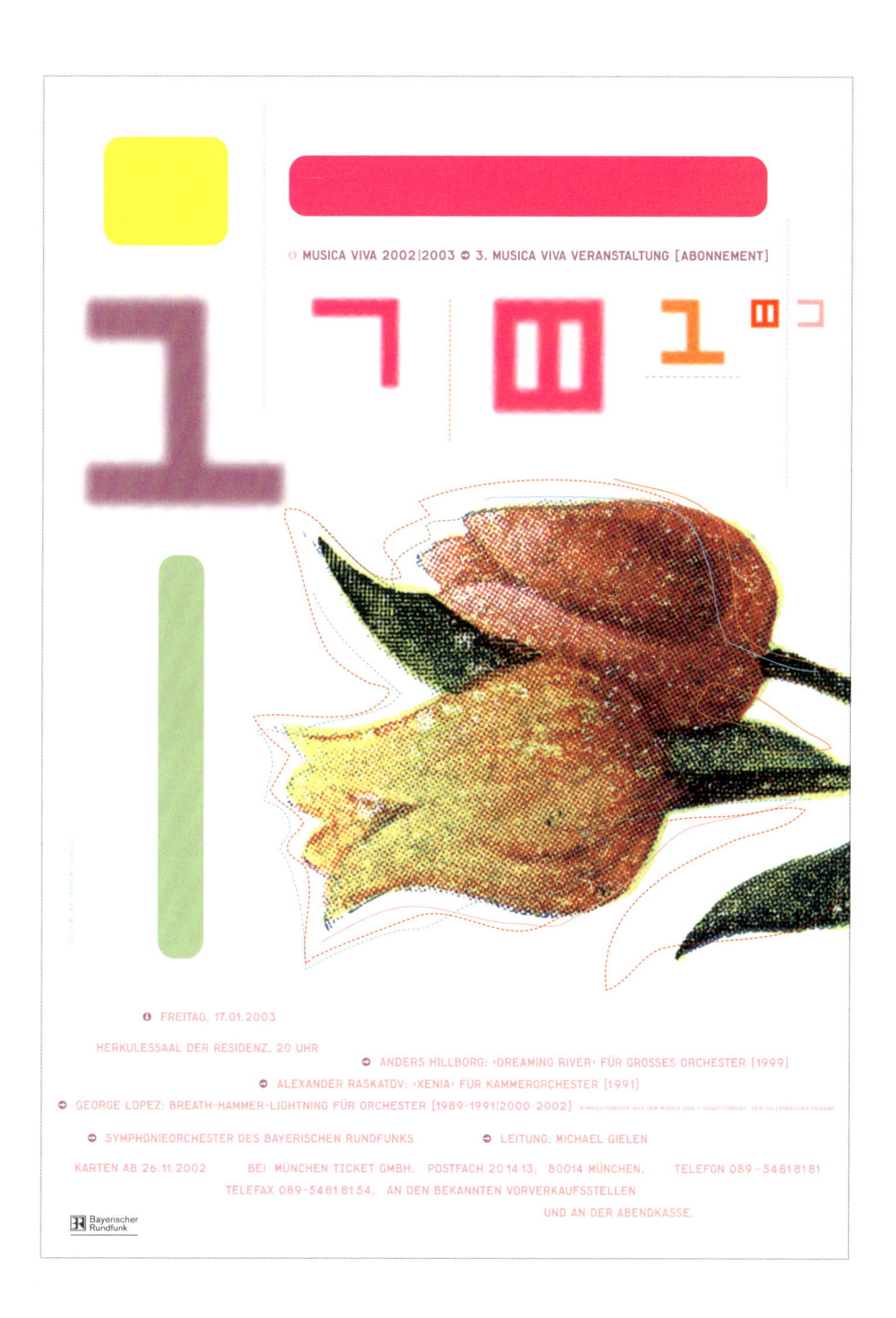

2002.03 04
Konzert > 26. Februar 2003
Wiesner, Milliken,
Kretzschmar, Thewes
A0 [841 x 1189 mm]

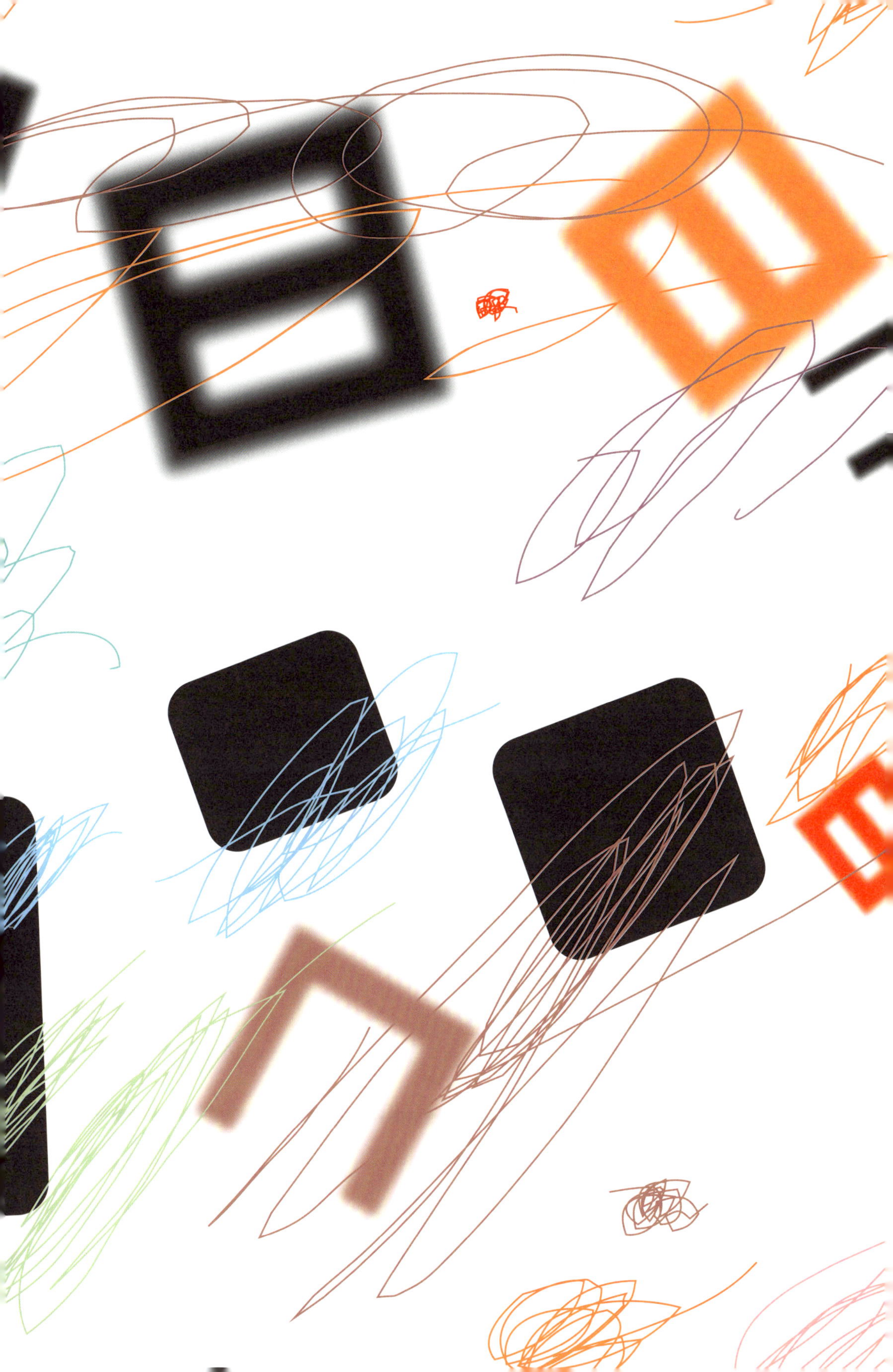

2002.03 05
Konzert > 28. März 2003
Poppe, Risset, Feiler,
Ablinger, Mello
A0 [841 x 1189 mm]

2002.03 07
Konzert > 6. Mai 2003
Ore, Reynolds, López, Hölszky
A0 [841 x 1189 mm]

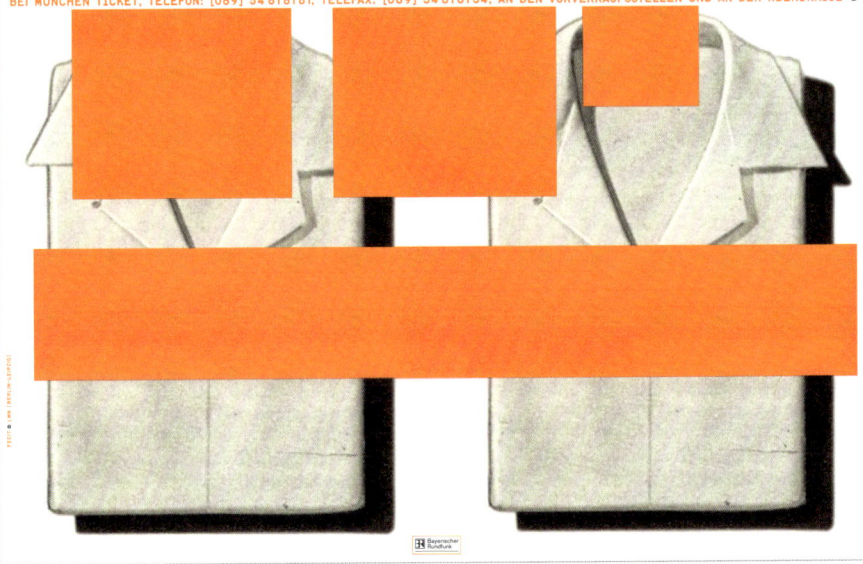

2002.03 06
Konzert > 29. April 2003
Sciarrino, Moon, Cassol
A0 [841 x 1189 mm]

2002.03 08
Konzert > 6. Juni 2003
Carlevaro, Sciarrino, Xenakis
A0 [841 x 1189 mm]

2002.03 09
Konzert > 11. Juli 2003
Skempton, Oehring, Ives
A0 [841 x 1189 mm]

musica viva präsentiert im herkulessaal der residenz münchen || 9. musica viva veranstaltung 2002|2003 am freitag, 11. juli 2003, 20 uhr, herkulessaal der residenz münchen || howard skempton ›konzert für drehleier, percussion und orchester‹ [1994] deutsche erstaufführung || helmut oehring ›das blaumeer‹ aus: ›einkehrtag‹ für sopran [männlich], solo e-gitarre, trompete und orchester [2002|2003] kompositionsauftrag der musica viva uraufführung || charles ives ›vierte symphonie‹ für chor, klavier und orchester [1910–1916] || drehleier: matthew spring || gitarre: jörg wilkendorff || sopran: arno raunig || trompete: william forman || klavier: barton weber || kodirigent: maxim heller || chor und symphonieorchester des bayerischen rundfunks || leitung: martyn brabbins || karten ab 20.05.2003 von 8.– bis 18.– € [schüler und studenten 8.– €] bei MÜNCHEN TICKET, Tel.: 0 89/54 81 81 81, Fax 0 89/ 54 81 81 54, sowie an den bekannten Vorverkaufsstellen und an der Abendkasse.

2003.04
offset print
CMYK + Pantone 803

2003.04 02
Konzert > 7. November 2003
Sannicandro, Dusapin, Eliasson
A0 [841 x 1189 mm]

2003.04 03
Konzert > 5. März 2004
Smutny, Lang, Mundry
A0 [841 x 1189 mm]

2003.04 04
Konzert > 23. März 2004
Donatoni, Lang, Barret, Berio
A0 [841 x 1189 mm]

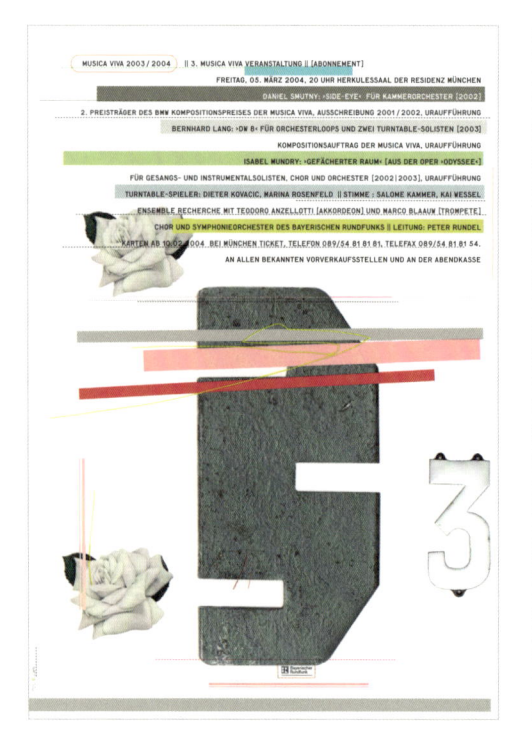

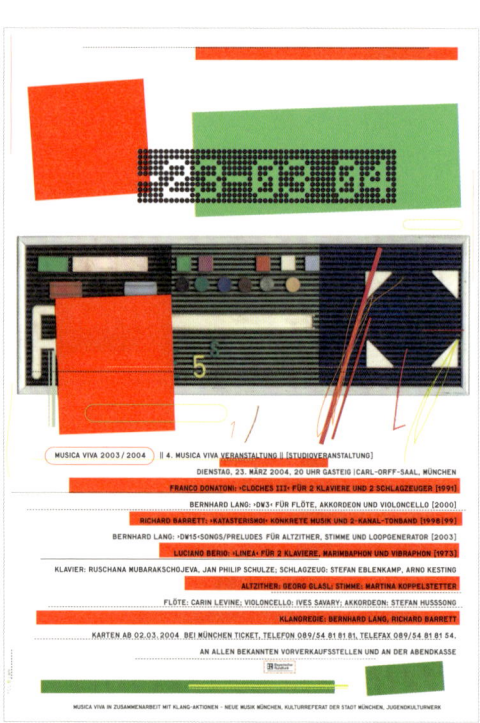

2003.04 05
Konzert > 2. April 2004
Nancarrow, Ligeti
A0 [841 x 1189 mm]

2003.04 06
Konzert > 16. April 2004
Widmann, Winkler, Haas,
Müller/Stache, Pagh-Paan
A0 [841 x 1189 mm]

2003.04 07
Konzert > 14. Mai 2004
Hillborg, Lindberg, Stucky, Salonen
A0 [841 x 1189 mm]

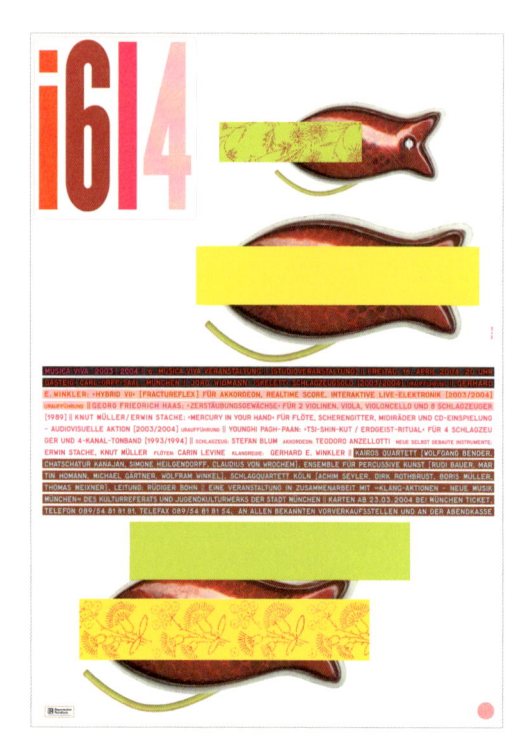

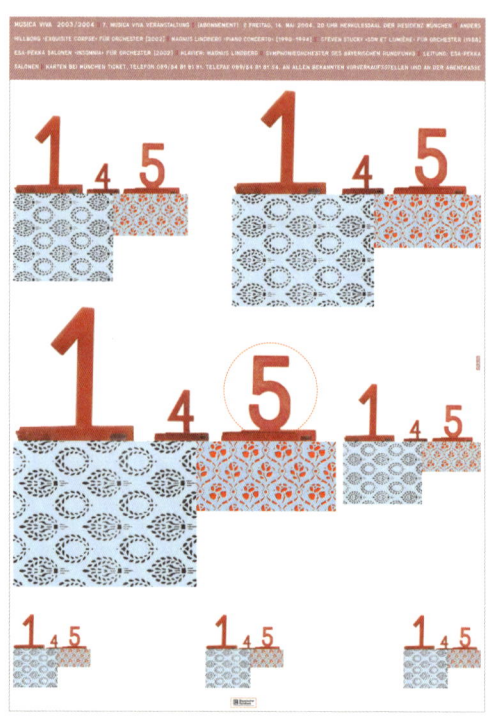

2003.04 08
Konzert > 12. Juni 2004
Rihm, Walter, Stäbler
A0 [841 x 1189 mm]

2003.04 09
Konzert > 9. Juli 2004
Donatoni, Haas, Nono
A0 [841 x 1189 mm]

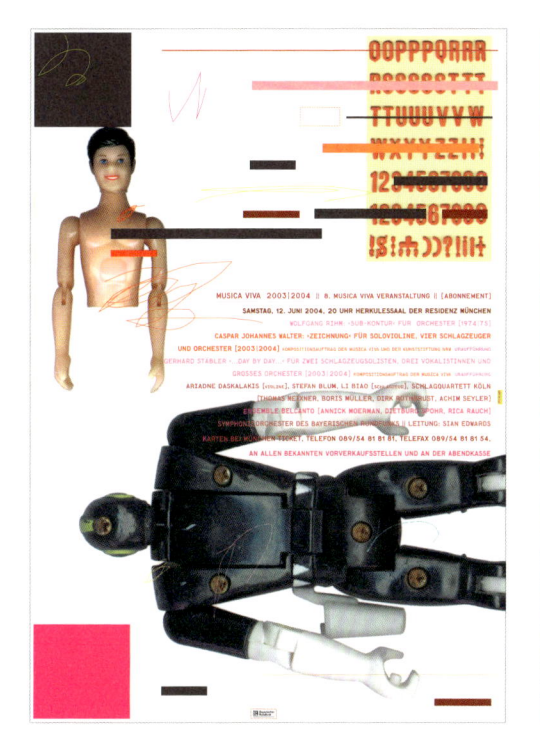

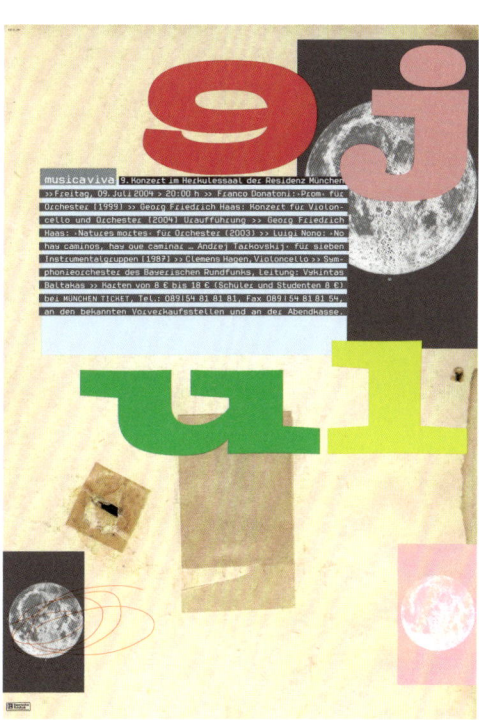

2004.05
offset print
CMYK + Pantone 803

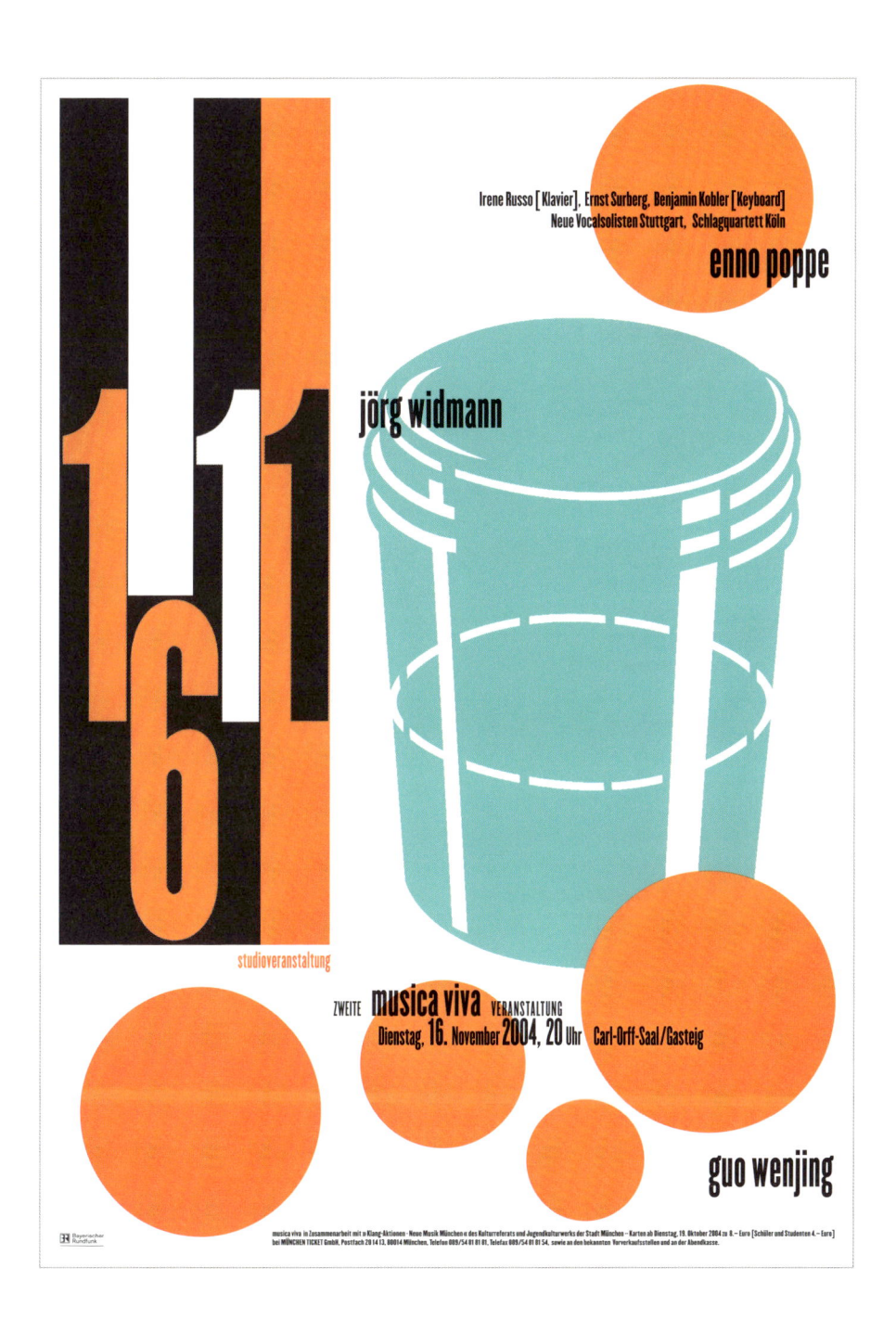

2004.05 02
Konzert > 16. November 2004
Poppe, Widmann, Wenjing
A1 [594 x 841 mm]

2004.05 03
Konzert > 11. Februar 2005
Wolf, Ingolfsson Xenakis, Huber
A1 [594 x 841mm]

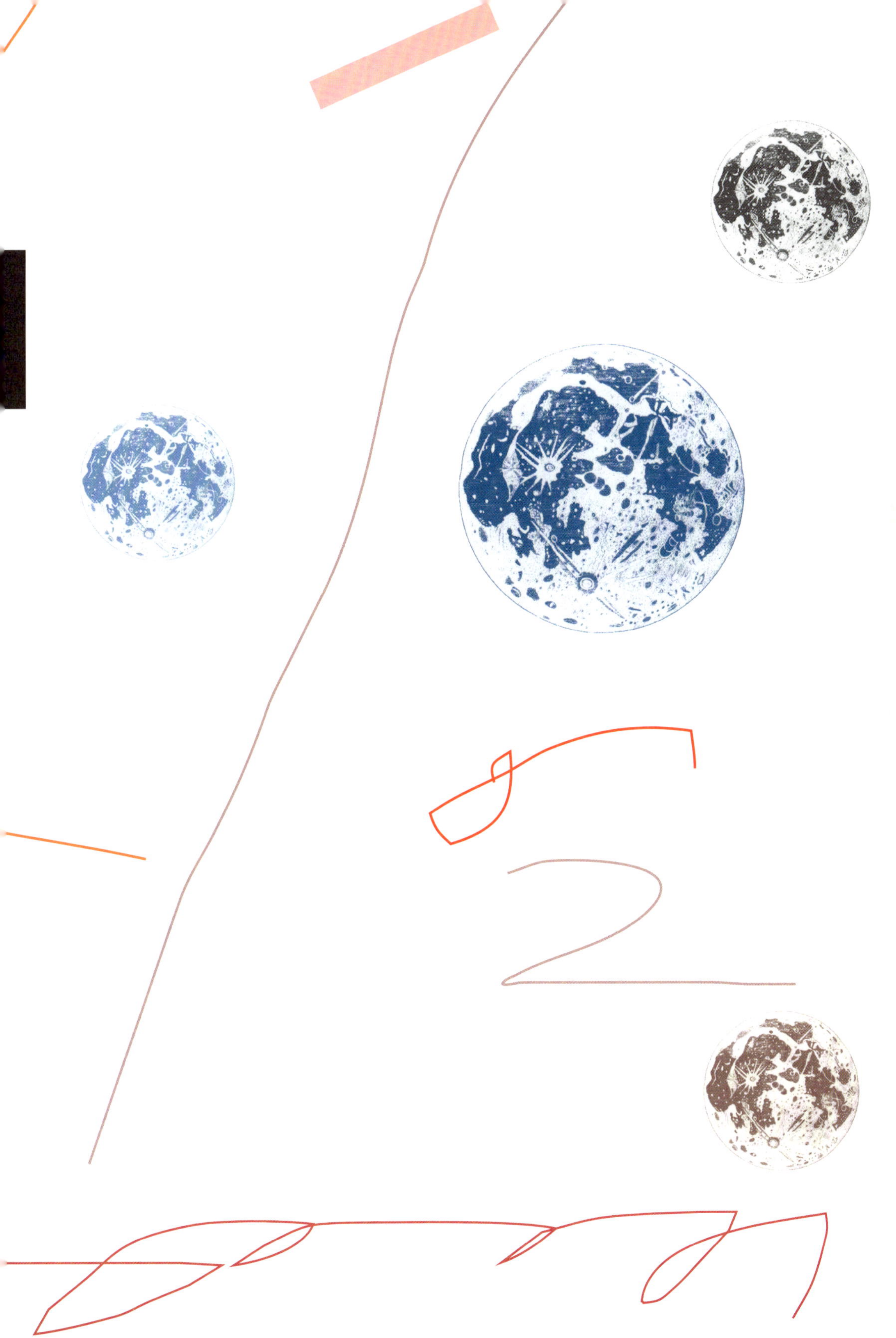
2

2004.05 04
Konzert > 21. Februar 2005
Schönberg, Höller, Carter, Boulez
A1 [594 x 841mm]

2004.05 05
Konzert > 11. März 2005
Lee Wong, Hölszky, Schnabel
A1 [594 x 841mm]

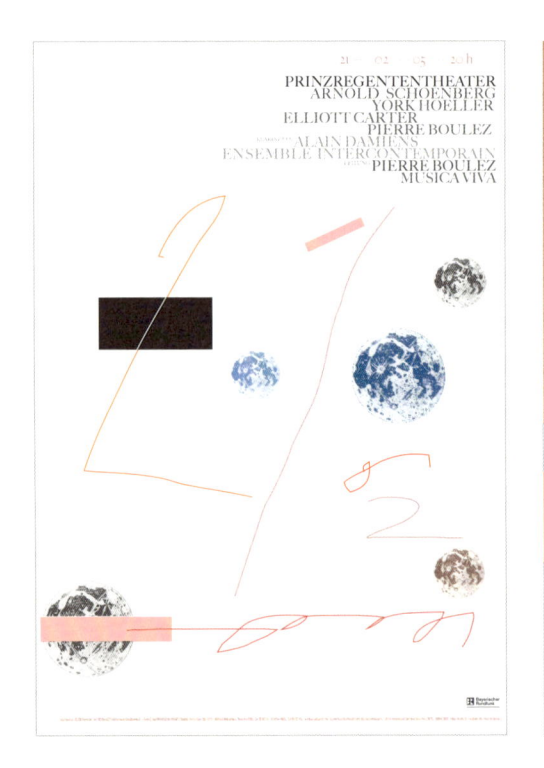

2004.05 06
Konzert > 15. April 2005
Barrett, Hirsch, Furrer, Schnebel
A1 [594 x 841mm]

2004.05 08
Konzert > 17. Juni 2005
Dillon, Lévy, André, Globokar
A1 [594 x 841mm]

2004.05 09
Konzert > 8. Juli 2005
Beaser, Narbutaite, Terterjan, Rouse
A1 [594 x 841mm]

2005.06
offset print
CMYK

2005.06 01
Konzert > 30. September 2005
Oehring, Hartmann, Henze
A1 [594 x 841mm]

2005.06 02
Konzert > 28. Oktober 2005
Zeller, Hartmann, von Schweinitz
A1 [594 x 841mm]

CONLON NANCARROW
GERARD GRISEY
GEORGE LOPEZ

2005.06 03
Konzert > 26. Januar 2006
Smolka, Eötvös, Heider
A1 [594 x 841 mm]

2005.06 04
Konzert > 6. Februar 2006
Nancarrow, Grisey, López
A1 [594 x 841mm]

2005.06 05
Konzert > 3. März 2006
Zender, Scelsi, Grisey
A1 [594 x 841mm]

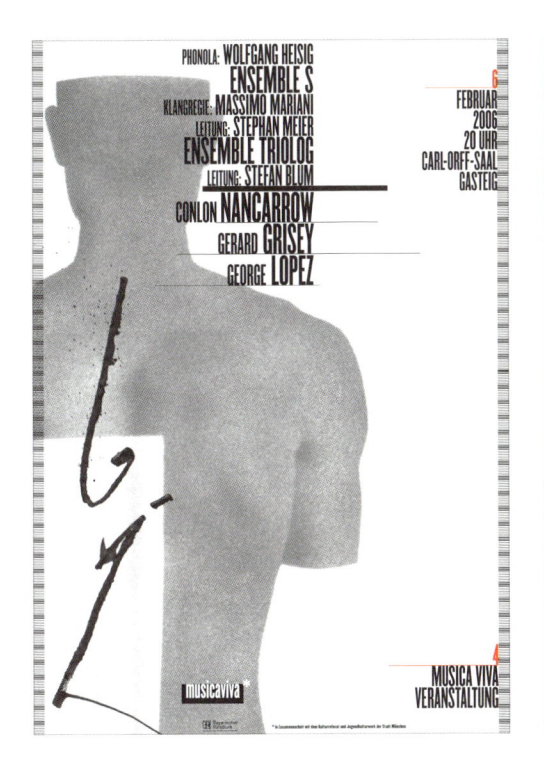

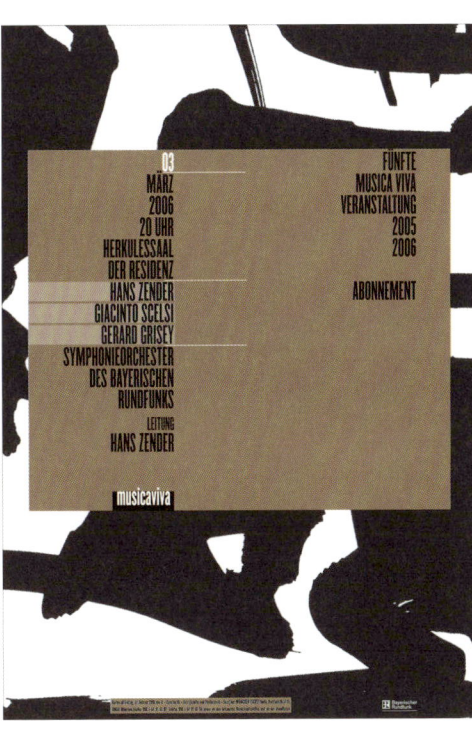

2005.06 08
Konzert > 26. Mai 2006
Katzer, Zimmermann, Nunes
A1 [594 x 841mm]

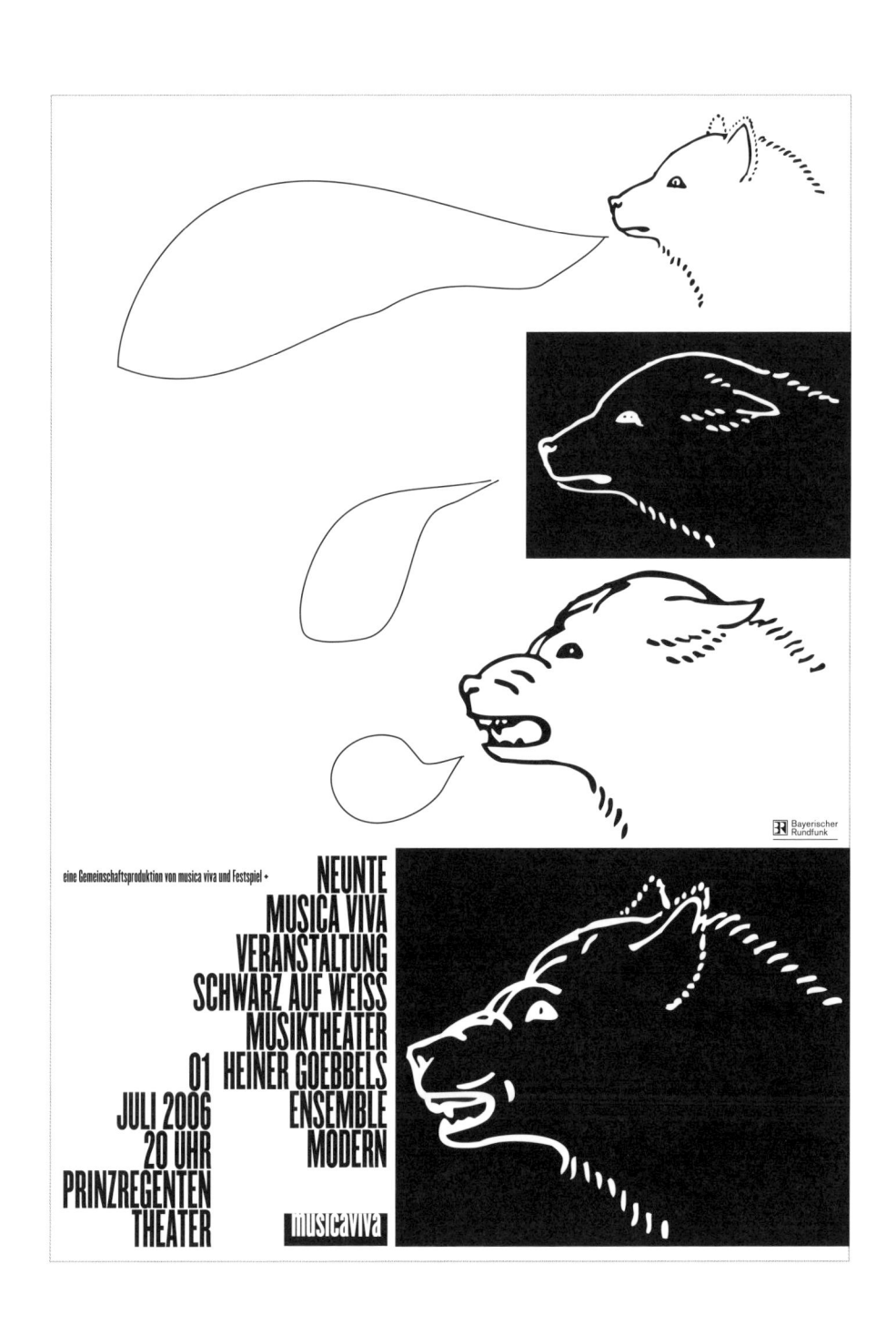

2005.06 09
Konzert > 1. Juli 2006
Goebbels
A1 [594 x 841 mm]

2006.07
offset print
CMYK + Gold

2006.07 01
Konzert > 1. Dezember 2006
Pelzel, Cerha, Sciarrino, Globokar
A1 [594 x 841mm]

2006.07 04
Konzert > 16. Februar 2007
Dufourt, Rihm, de Oliveira,
Odeh-Tamimi, Xenakis,
A1 [594 x 841mm]

2006.07 07
Konzert > 11. Mai 2007
Dittrich, Lee Wong, Wenjing
A1 [594 x 841mm]

2006.07 08
Konzert > 27. Juni 2007
PASSPORT
Andovska, Azarova, Fabian, Lemke
A1 [594 x 841mm]

2006.07 09
Konzert > 6. Juli 2007
Bialas, Koch, Tenney, Villanueva
A1 [594 x 841mm]

2007.08
offset print
CMYK
silk screen print [Edition]
black

2007.08 02
Konzert > 14. Dezember 2007
Andre, Brass, Haas
A1 [594 x 841 mm]

2007.08 F2
FESTIVAL > 25. Jan. – 15. Feb. 2008
Stockhausen, Hartmann, Zender, Czernowin,
Hölszky, Widmann, Lang, Lim, Lentz
A1 [594 x 841mm]

2007.08 03
Konzert > 4. April 2008
Xenakis, Mahnkopf, Feiler
A1 [594 x 841mm]
Edition 20 Ex. [1000 x 1400 mm]

2008.09
offset print
CMYK + Pantone 803

2008.09 01
Konzert > 17. Oktober 2008
de Gelmini, Tsangaris, Dohmen
A1 [594 x 841mm]

2008.09 03
Konzert > 9. Januar 2009
Stordeur, Grosskopf, Beyer, Smutny
A1 [594 x 841mm]

2008.09 04
Konzert > 6. Februar 2009
Kim, Veerhoff, Pagh-Paan, Odeh-Tamimi
A1 [594 x 841mm]

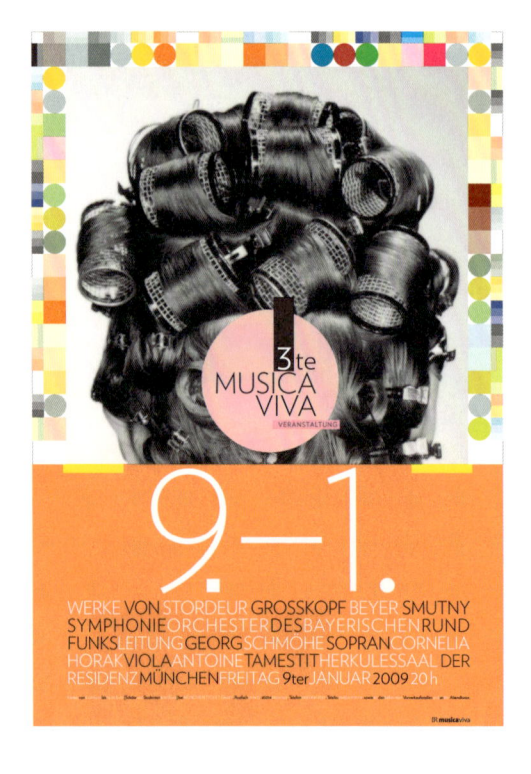

786

2008.09 05
Konzert > 6. März 2009
Schnebel, Fujikura
A1 [594 x 841mm]

2008.09 08
Konzert > 18. Juni 2009
Globokar, Hamel, Wertmüller
A1 [594 x 841mm]

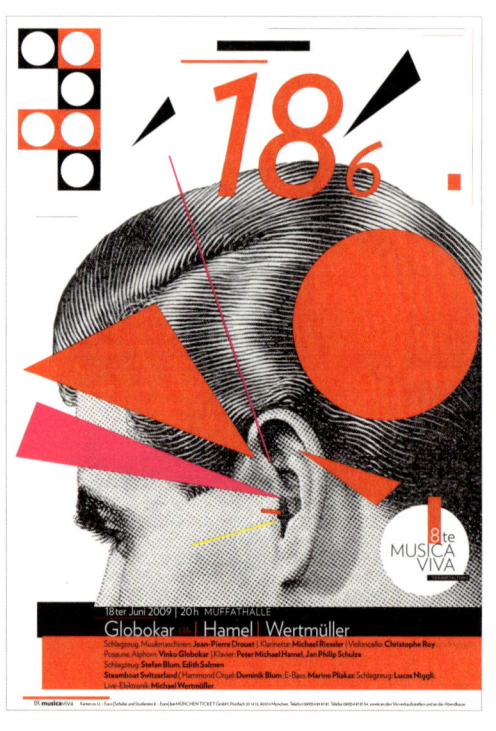

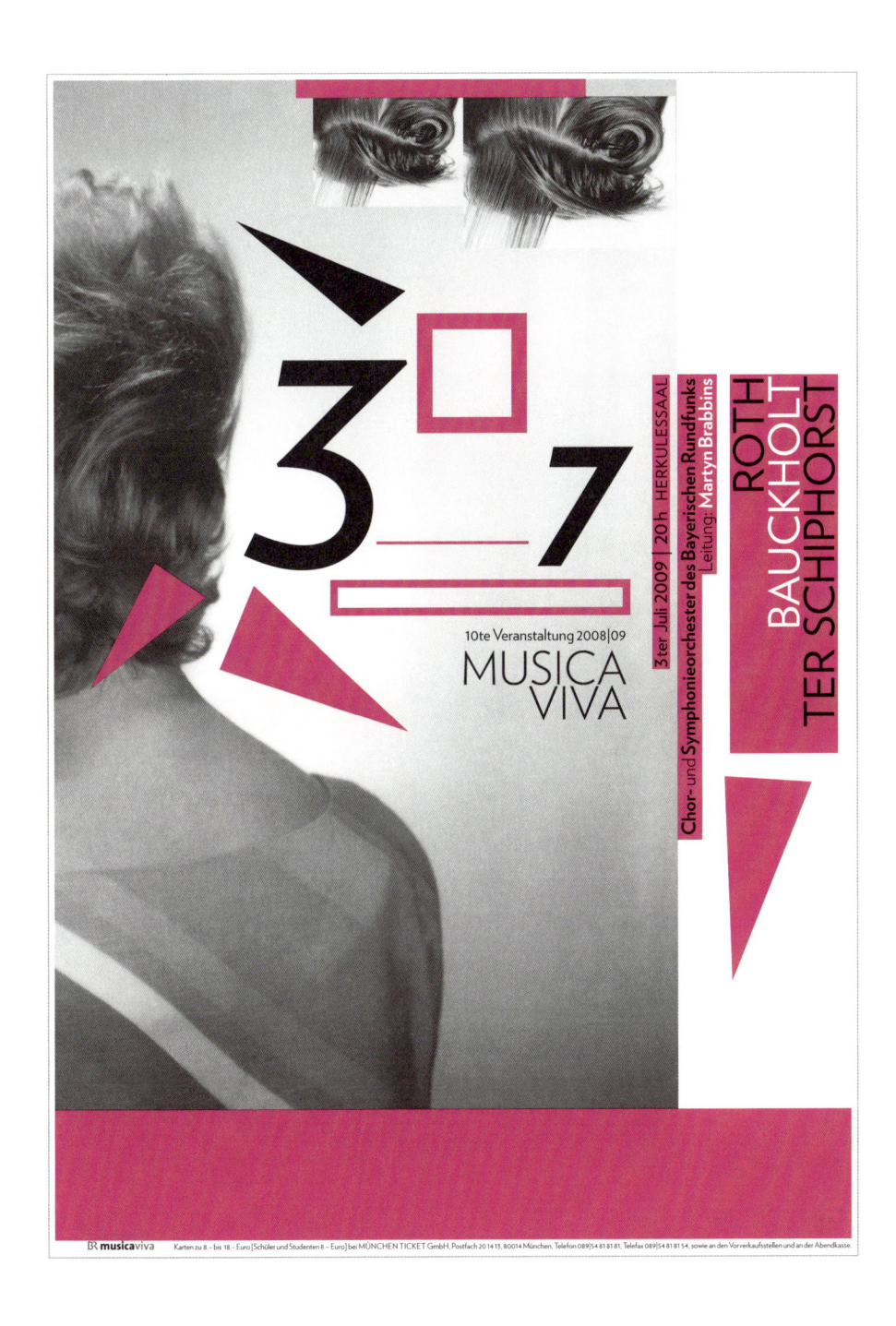

2008.09 09
Konzert > 3. Juli 2009
Roth, Bauckholt, ter Schiphorst
A1 [594 x 841mm]

2009.10
offset print
CMYK

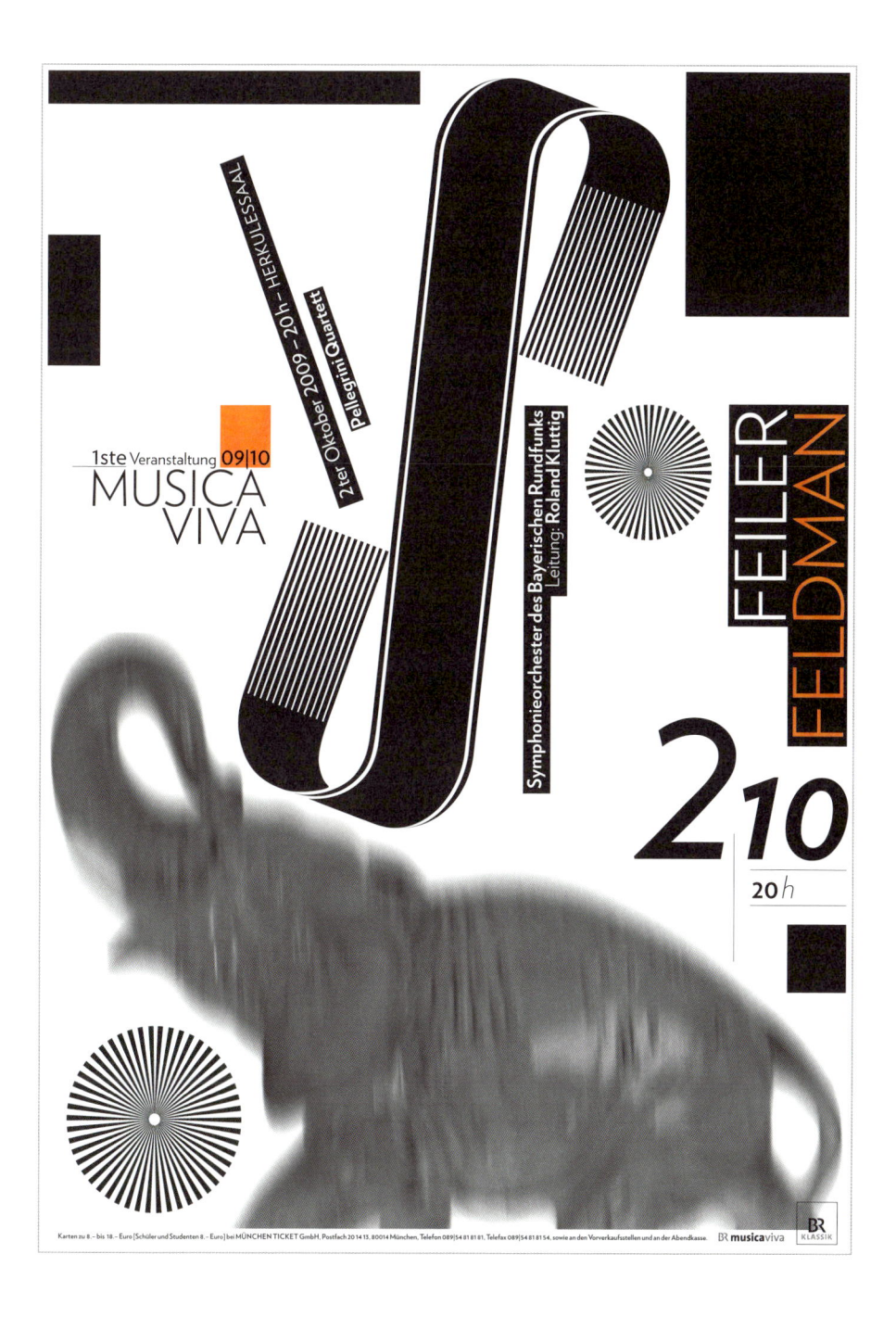

2009.10 01
Konzert > 2. Oktober 2009
Feiler, Feldman
A1 [594 x 841 mm]

2009.10 02
Konzert > 27. Oktober 2009
Newski, Netti, Poppe, Riedl
A1 [594 x 841 mm]

2010

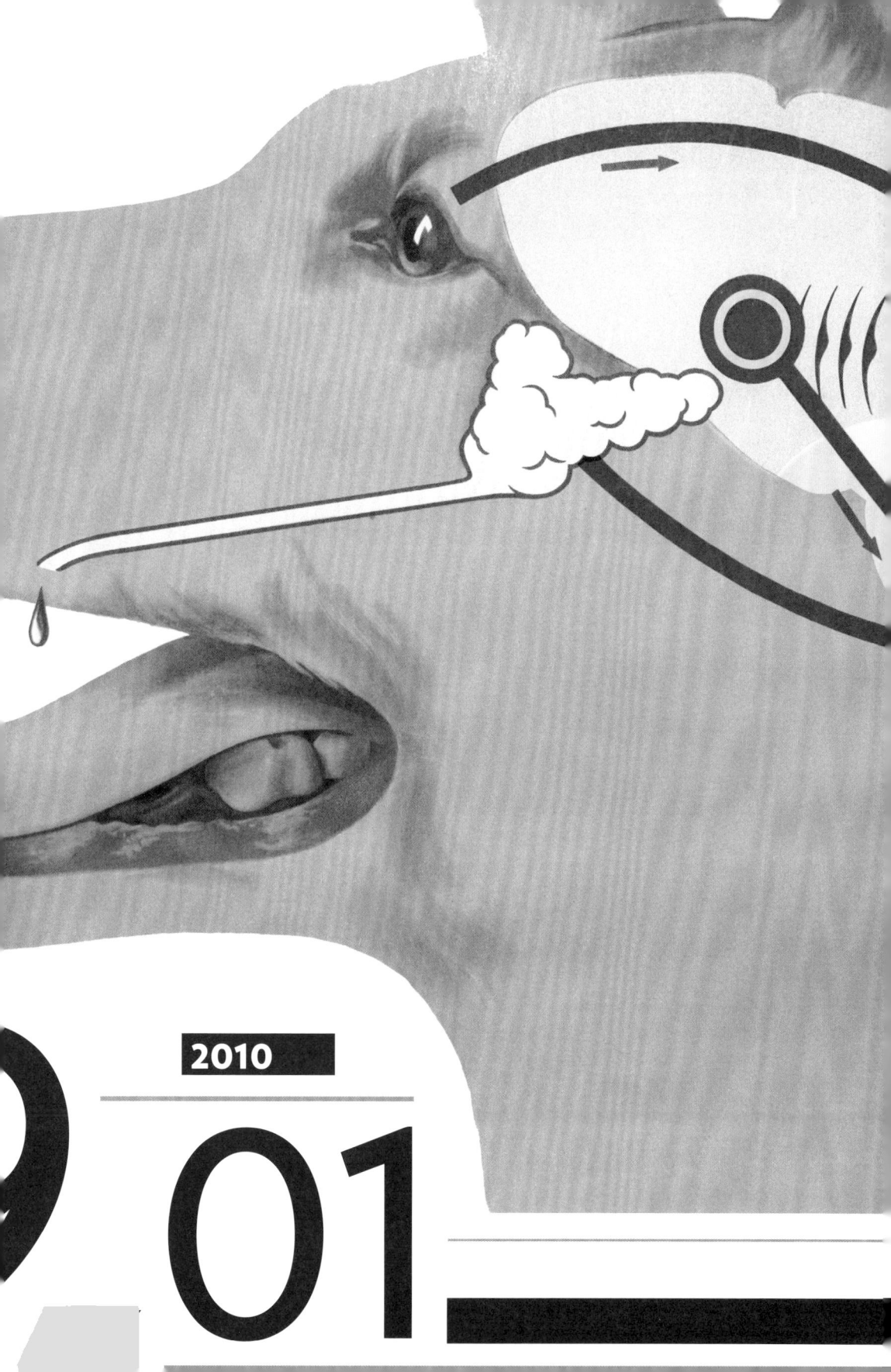

01

2009.10 03
Konzert > 19. Januar 2010
Wolf, Poppe/Heiniger, Hirsch
A1 [594 x 841 mm]

2009.10 04
Konzert > 15. Februar 2010
Eggert, Schnebel, Pauset
A1 [594 x 841 mm]

2009.10 05
Konzert > 17. März 2010
Oehring
A1 [594 x 841mm]

2009.10 06
Konzert > 23. April 2010
Trojahn, Dusapin, Widmann, Donatoni
A1 [594 x 841 mm]

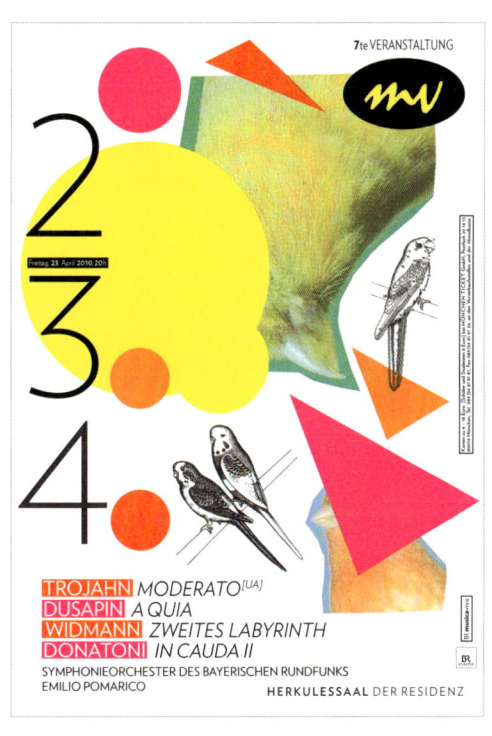

2009.10 07
Konzert > 4. Juni 2010
Winkler, Oehring, Dittrich
A1 [594 x 841mm]

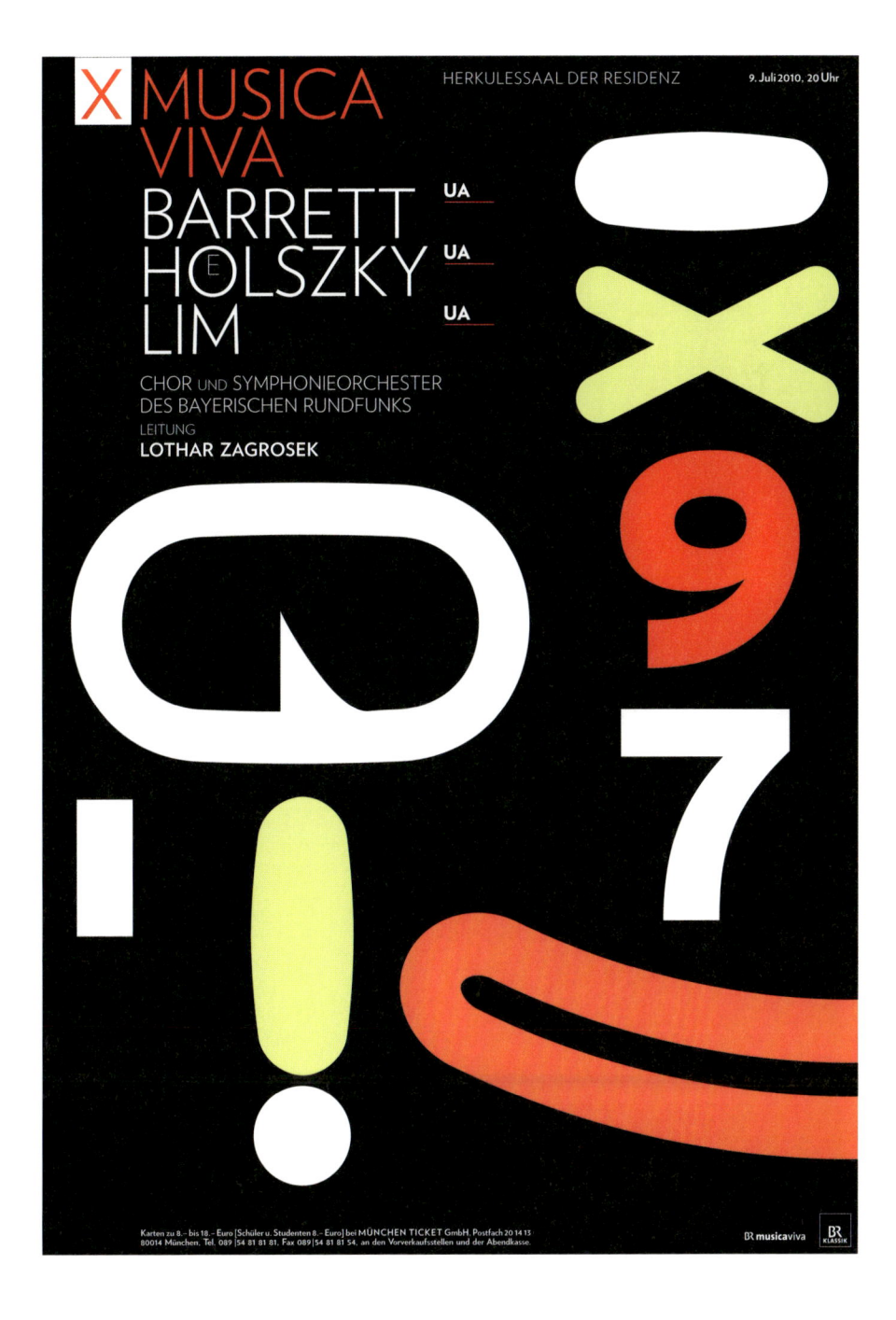

2009.10 09
Konzert > 9. Juli 2010
Barrett, Hölszky, Lim
A1 [594 x 841mm]

2010.11
offset print
CMYK + Pantone 806, 803

2010.11 01
Konzert > 24. September 2010
Urbanner, Sora, Stroppa, Baltakas
A1 [594 x 841mm]

2010.11 02
Konzert > 11. November 2010
Mochizuki, Heiniger, Poppe, Furrer
A1 [594 x 841mm]

2010.11 03
Konzert > 11. Februar 2011
Czernowin, Schenker, Koch, Tenney
A1 [594 x 841mm]

2010.11 04
Konzert > 4. März 2011
Herchet, Sannicandro,
Kupsch, Romitelli
A1 [594 x 841mm]

2010.11 05
Konzert > 7. April 2011
Dillon, Hübler, Ferneyhough,
Billone, Dufourt
A1 [594 x 841mm]

2010.11 06
Konzert > 27. Mai 2011
de Gelmini, Nakatani,
Franke, Hartmann
A1 [594 x 841mm]

2010.11 07
Konzert > 8. Juli 2011
Lachenmann, Zender, Zimmermann
A1 [594 x 841mm]

2011.12
offset print
CMYK

2011.12 01
Konzert > 30. September 2011
Boulez
A1 [594 x 841mm]

2011.12 02
Konzert > 28. Oktober 2011
Pousseur, Cage, Berio, Ives
A1 [594 x 841mm]

2011.12 03
Konzert > 14. Dezember 2011
Boulez
A1 [594 x 841mm]

2011.12 04
Konzert > 17. Dezember 2011
Cage
A1 [594 x 841mm]

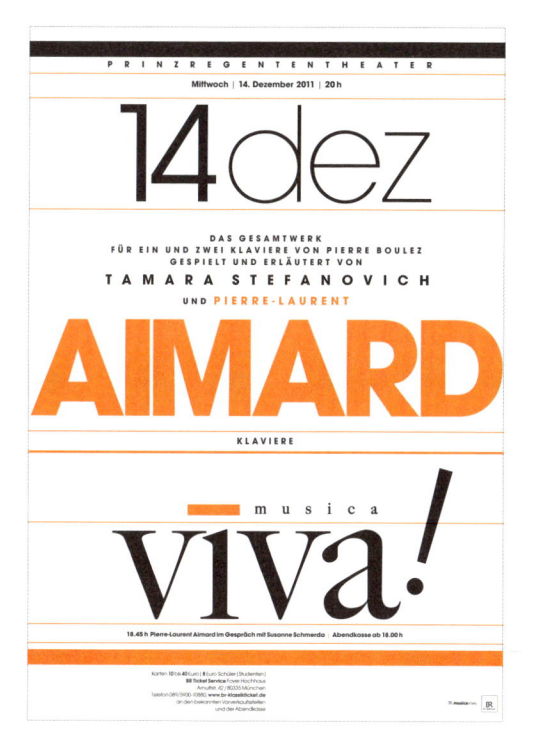

2011.12 05
Konzert > 14. Januar 2012
Messiaen, Carter, Pagh-Paan
A1 [594 x 841 mm]

2011.12 06
Konzerte > 16./17. Februar 2012
Moguillansky, Mendoza, Schüttler,
Hurt/Prins/Poppe, Ives, Birtwistle
A1 [594 x 841mm]

2011.12 07
Konzert > 4. Mai 2012
Ligeti, Murail, Messiaen, Benjamin
A1 [594 x 841mm]

2011.12 08
Konzert > 15. Juni 2012
Haas, Rihm
A1 [594 x 841 mm]

2011.12 09
Konzert > 16. Juni 2012
Lazkano, Brass, López
A1 [594 x 841mm]

2012.13
offset print
CMYK

2012.13 04
Konzert > 22. Februar 2013
Andre, Mundry, Hartmann
A1 [594 x 841mm]

DIN A1 hoch   Text für Plakat 22.02.13

Mark **Andre**
... hij...
Isabel **Mundry**
Non-Places,
ein Klavierkonzert |* UA
Karl Amadeus **Hartmann**
7. Symphonie
musica viva
Freitag, 22. Februar 2013 20:00 H
München
Telefon 089/5900-10880
www.br-klassikticket.de
Herkulessaal der Residenz
Nicolas Hodges, Klavier
Symphonieorchester
des Bayerischen Rundfunks
Emilio Pomarico, Leitung

*|Kompositionsauftrag der musica viva
des Bayerischen Rundfunks
in Verbindung mit dem Happy New Ears-Komponistenpreis 2013
der Hans und Gertrud Zender-Stiftung

DU-Abgabe 28.01.2013

GÜNTER KARL BOSE

Logo BR Klassik
Logo musica viva

2012.13 05
Konzert > 26. April 2013
Sciarrino, Saunders, Lachenmann
A1 [594 x 841mm]

2012.13 S
OPER > 26. Juni – 1. Juli 2013
Stockhausen
SAMSTAG aus LICHT
A1 [594 x 841 mm]
A0 [841 x 1189 mm]

2013.14
offset print
CMYK

2013.14 01
Konzert > 8. November 2013
Pesson, Manoury
[Foto: Benjamin Rinner]
A1 [594 x 841mm]

2013.14 02
Konzert > 15. November 2013
Adámek, Barry, Feldman
[Foto: Benjamin Rinner]
A1 [594 x 841mm]

2013.14 03
Konzert > 13. Dezember 2013
Zorn, López, Manoury
[Foto: Benjamin Rinner]
A1 [594 x 841mm]

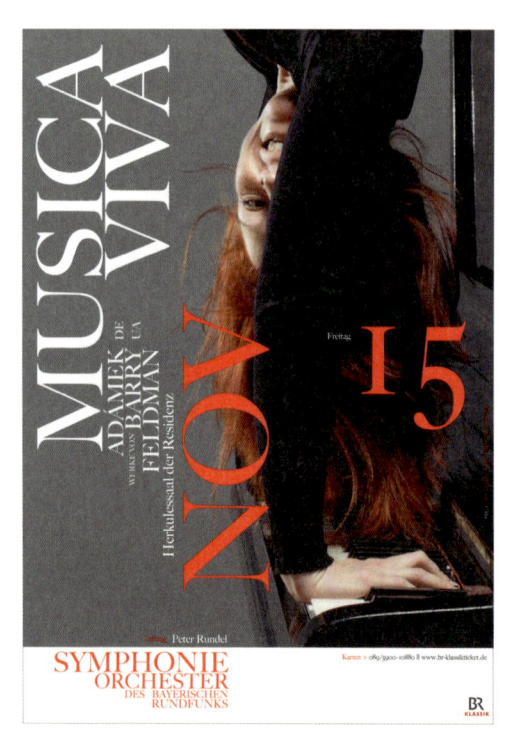

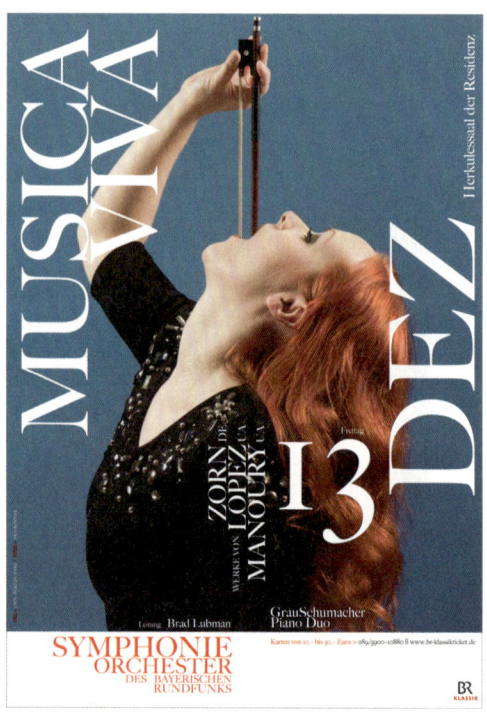

2013.14 06
Konzert > 6. Juni 2014
Johnson, Lang, Richter de Vroe
[Foto: Benjamin Rinner]
A1 [594 x 841mm]

2014.15
offset print
CMYK+Pantone 803 / 810

zuhören ist eine tätigkeit!

Abonnementpreise

2014.15 A
Abonnementwerbung
A1 [594 x 841 mm]

2014.15 01
Konzert > 24. Oktober 2014
Herrmann, Stroppa, Birtwistle
A1 [594 x 841 mm]

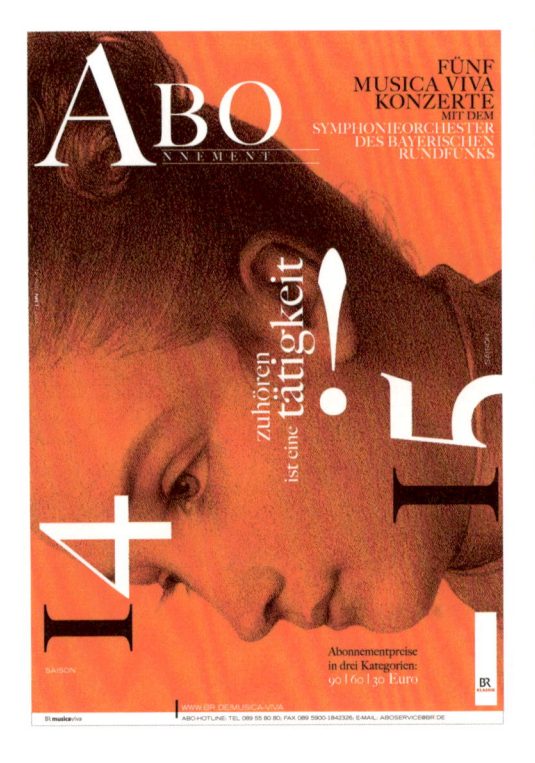

2014.15 02
Konzert > 12. Dezember 2014
Pelzel, Andre, Smolka
[Objekt: Daniel Wittner]
A1 [594 x 841 mm]

2014.15 03
Konzerte > 19. – 21. Februar 2015
Djordjević, Richter de Vroe, Sabat,
Skrzypczak, Bella, Saunders, Globokar,
Partch, Zappa
[Objekt: Daniel Wittner]
A1 [594 x 841mm]

2014.15 04
Konzert > 20. März 2015
Castiglioni, Filidei, Aperghis
[Objekt: Daniel Wittner]
A1 [594 x 841mm]

2014.15 05
Konzert > 8. Mai 2015
Srnka, Poppe, Spahlinger, Ligeti
[Objekte: Daniel Wittner, Felix Holler]
A1 [594 x 841mm]

2015.16
offset print
Black + Pantone 811, 812

2015.16 02
Konzert > 4. Dezember 2015
Widmann, Milliken, Reich
A1 [594 x 841 mm]

2015.16 03
Konzert > 22. Januar 2016
Verunelli, Manoury, Mundry, Busoni
A1 [594 x 841 mm]

2015.16 04
Konzerte > 26. / 27. Februar 2016
Saunders, Aperghis, Wolpe
Tallis, Feldman, di Lasso, Desprez
Benjamin, Boulez, Ligeti, Haas
A1 [594 x 841 mm]

2015.16 05
Konzerte > 3. – 5. Juni 2016
Reich, Eggert, Riedl
A1 [594 x 841 mm]

2016.17
offset print
Black + Pantone 803, 810, 811, 813

2016.17 01
Konzert > 7. Oktober 2016
Zender
A1 [594 x 841 mm]

2016.17 03
Konzerte > 30. März – 1. April 2017
Rihm, Xenakis, Vivier, Berio
A1 [594 x 841 mm]

2016.17 04
Konzerte > 30. März – 1. April 2017
Rihm, Xenakis, Vivier, Berio
A0 [1189 x 841 mm]

2016.17 06
Konzert > 2. Juni 2017
Bianchi, Thomalla, Grisey
A1 [594 x 841 mm]

2016.17 07
Konzerte > 6. / 8. Juli 2017
Andre, Sciarrino, Birtwistle,
Rihm, Harvey
A1 [594 x 841 mm]

2016.17 08
Konzert > 7. Juli 2017
Andre, Pintscher, Kurtág, Harvey
A1 [594 x 841 mm]

2016.17 09
Imageplakat > Saison 17/18
18/1 Großfläche [3560 x 2520 mm]

2016.17 10
Imageplakat > Saison 17/18
18/1 Großfläche [3560 x 2520 mm]

GRISEY

HECHTLE
WINKLER
BERTRAND
ADAMEK
LACHENMANN
SAUNDERS
BENJAMIN

APERGHIS

iva.de
(ührenfrei)

2016.17 11
Imageplakat > Saison 17/18
18/1 Großfläche [3560 x 2520 mm]

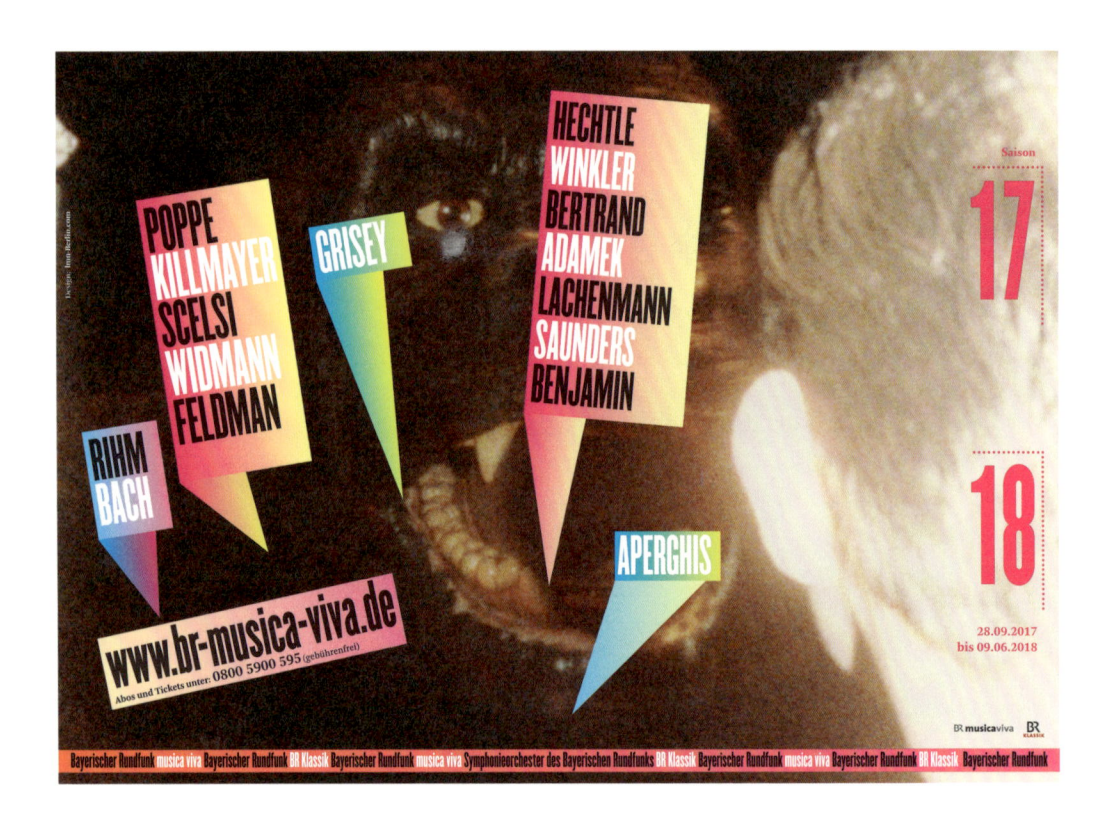

1997–2017
Synposis / synposis

1997–2017
Synposis / synposis

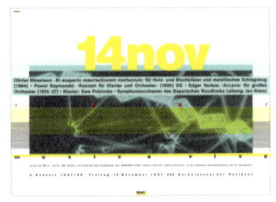

1997.98

01 02 03
04 05 06
07 08 09

1998.99

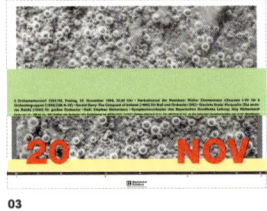

01 02 03
04 05 06

1997–2017
Synposis / synposis

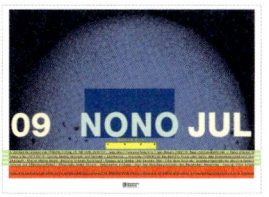

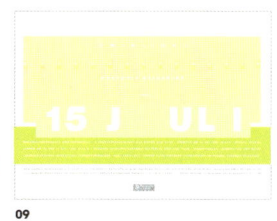

1999.00

2000.01

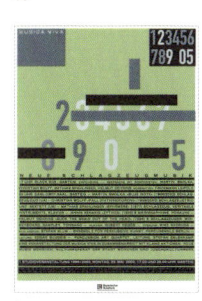

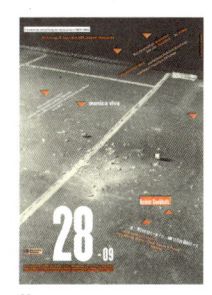

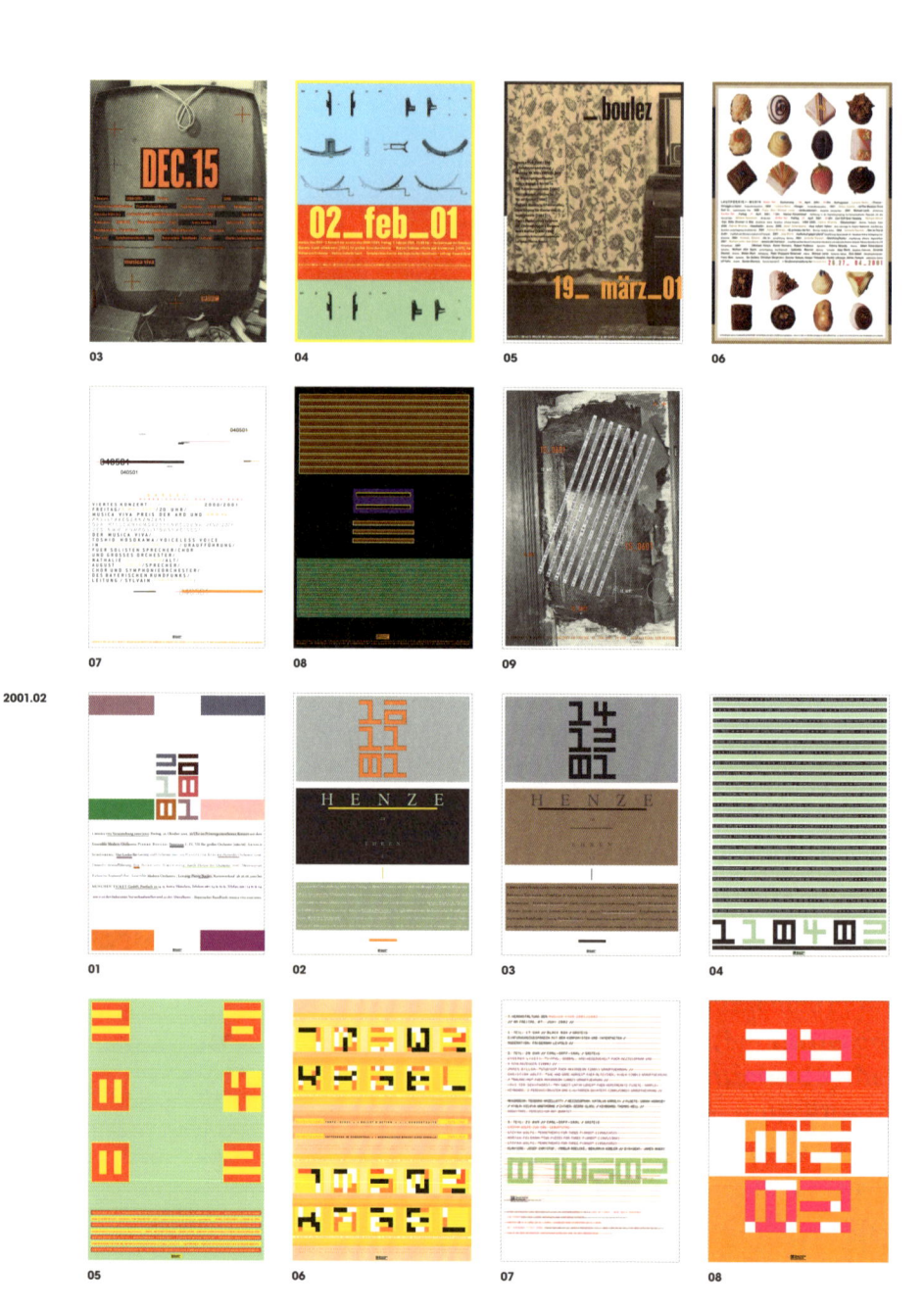

1997–2017
Synposis / synposis

2001.02

1997 – 2017
Synposis / synposis

2002.03

09

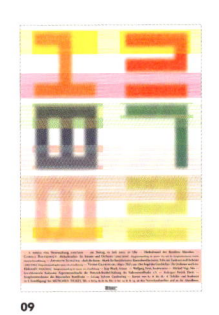

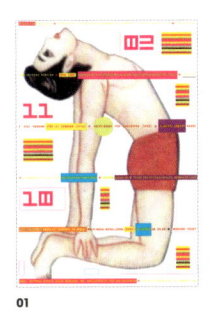

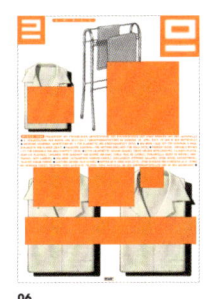

03 04 05 06

07 08 09

2003.04

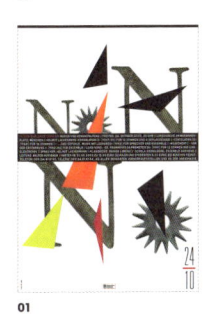

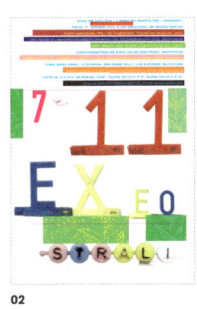

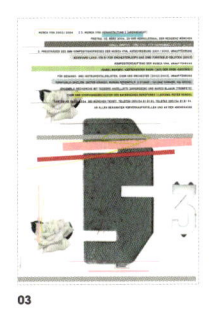

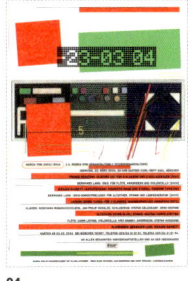

01 02 03 04

1997–2017
Synposis / synposis

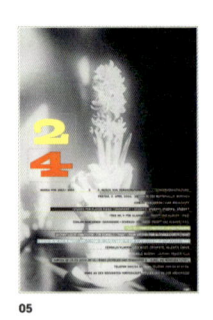

2004.05

05
06 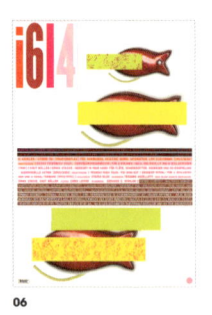
07 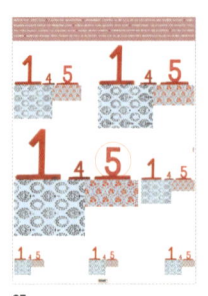
08 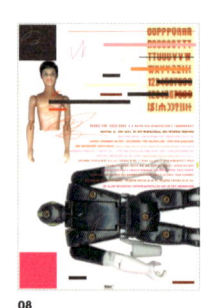
09 
01
02 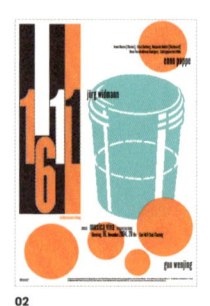
03 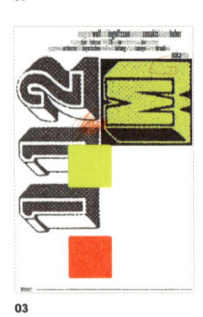
04 
05 
06 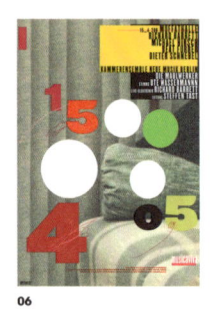
07
08 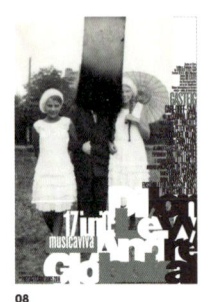
09

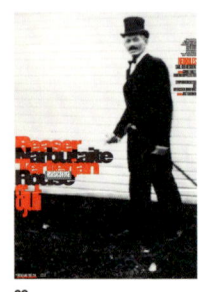

1997–2017
Synposis / synposis

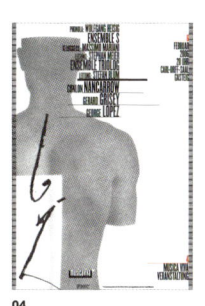

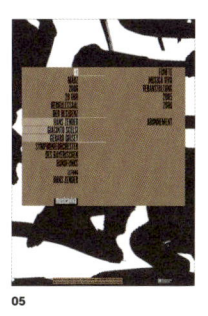

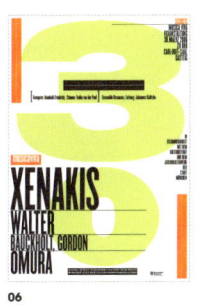

2005.06

01 02 03 04

05 06 07 08

2006.07

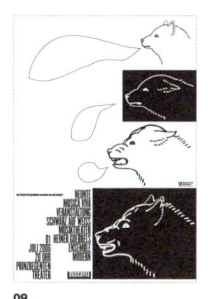

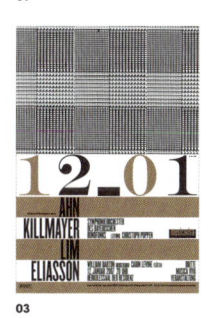

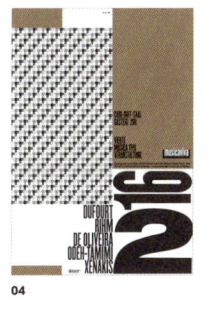

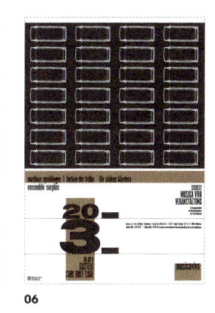

09 01 02

03 04 05 06

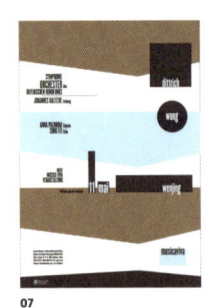

1997–2017
Synposis / synposis

07 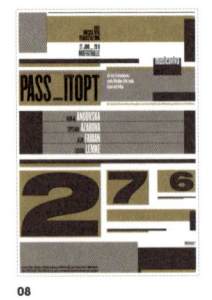 08  09

2007.08

01 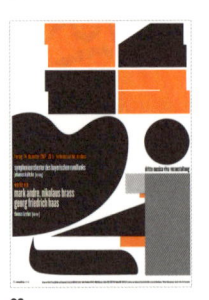 02 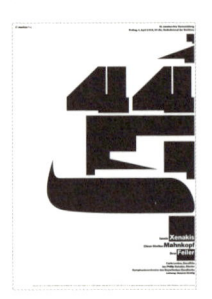 03  04

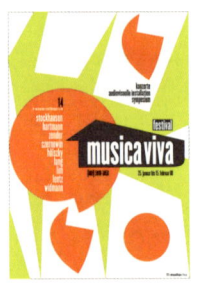

F1  F2 2008.09 01

02  03  04  05

1997– 2017
Synposis / synposis

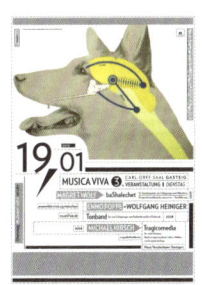

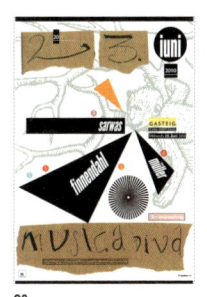

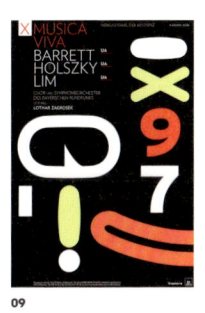

2009.10

06
07
08
09

01
02
03
04

05
06
07
08

2010.11

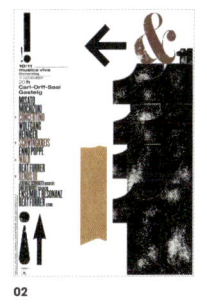

09
01
02

1997–2017
Synposis / synposis

2011.12

03
04 
05 
06 
07 
01
02 
03 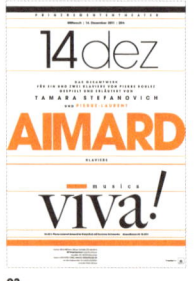
04 
05 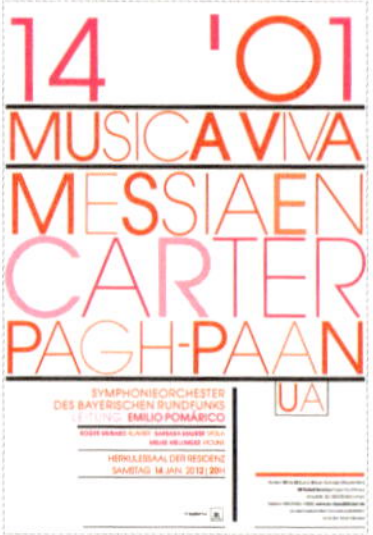
06 
07 
08 
09

1997–2017

Synposis / synposis

2012.13

01 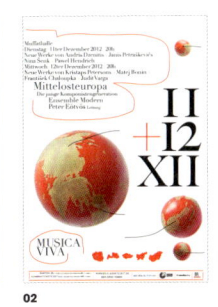 02  03  04

05  S 2013.14 01

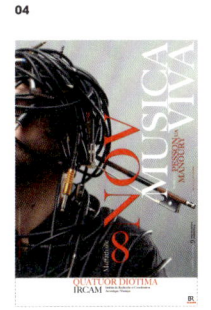

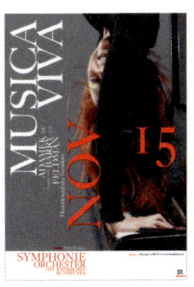

02  03  04  05

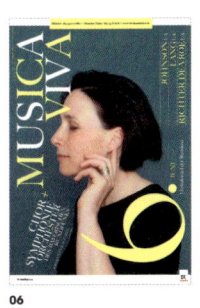

06 2014.15 A  01

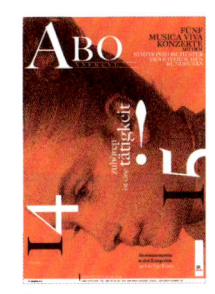

1997–2017
Synposis / synposis

02    03 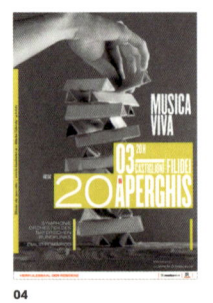   04    05

2015.16

01    02    03

2016.17 
04   05   01

02 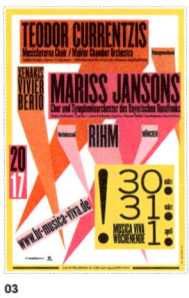   03    04

1997 – 2017

Synposis / synposis

05

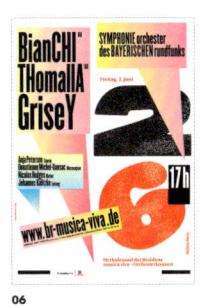

06

07

08

09

10

11

Anita Kühnel:

Mut zu neuen Formulierungen.
Günter Karl Boses Arbeiten
für die *musica viva*

Der Schweizer Armin Hofmann nannte das Wirkungsfeld des Grafikers eine besondere Klangwelt, die aus der Verbindung von Bild und Schrift entsteht, und schrieb: »Die harmonische Verbindung von zwei verschiedenartigen Systemen setzt notwendigerweise eine Vertiefung des künstlerischen Empfindens und Mut zu neuen Gedankengängen und Formulierungen voraus.«

Als ich im Jahr 2008 von Berlin nach München reiste, begegnete ich unweit vom Bahnhof zum ersten Mal einem *musica viva*-Plakat an der Litfaßsäule. Die ungewöhnlichen schwarzen, zunächst etwas kryptisch anmutenden Formen zogen mich in ihren Bann, weil sie wie Ausrufezeichen über den weiten weißen Papierraum triumphierten, auf dem sie gedruckt waren. Mit diesem wunderbaren Willkommensgruß präsentierte sich nicht nur die Kulturstadt München, der Bayerische Rundfunk als Veranstalter einer bedeutenden Konzertreihe der Moderne und Avantgarde, sondern auch die eigenwillige Stimme eines Grafikers, für den die Worte Armin Hofmanns geradezu als Programm stehen könnten.

Seit nunmehr 20 Jahren wirbt Günter Karl Bose mit Plakaten, Programmheften und Postkarten für das ambitionierte Konzertprogramm der *musica viva*. Die sich bis heute dem musikalischen Schaffen der Gegenwart widmende Konzertreihe besteht seit über 70 Jahren. Als weltweit beachtete Institution ist sie der lebendigen Tradition der Förderung gegenwärtigen Musikschaffens verpflichtet, getreu des von ihrem Gründervater postulierten Mottos: »Musik ist eine Sprache der Gegenwart«. Seit Oktober 1945 initiierte der Komponist und gerade zum Dramaturgen der Bayerischen Staatstheater berufene Karl Amadeus Hartmann mit Unterstützung der amerikanischen Militärverwaltung regelmäßige Konzerte zeitgenössischer Musik – zunächst mit dem Bayerischen Staatsorchester –, die ab Juli 1947 den Namen »musica viva« trugen. Ab 1948 fanden dann die Konzerte in Verbindung mit »Radio München« statt, wie der Bayerische Rundfunk damals noch hieß. Als 1949 das Symphonieorchester des Bayerischen Rundfunks gegründet wurde, wurde auch Karl Amadeus Hartmanns *musica viva*-Konzertreihe dem Bayerischen Rundfunk integriert und das Symphonieorchester wurde ihr fester und stärkster Partner: Zahllose *musica viva*-Auftragskompositionen hat das Symphonieorchester seither zur Uraufführung gebracht, vom Bayerischen Rundfunk produziert und für eine große Öffentlichkeit aus dem Konzertsaal in seinen Sendeprogrammen von BR-Klassik vermittelt und übertragen. Die Lebendigkeit der musikalischen Gegenwartssprache sollte sich nicht zuletzt auch stets in dem werbenden und einladenden Erscheinungsbild niederschlagen. So wie die *musica viva* unterschiedlichsten musikalischen Temperamenten ihre Bühne zur Verfügung stellte, so hat sie auch von Beginn an den grafischen Gestaltern ihrer Publikationen freien Raum für die Entfaltung der bildnerischen Sprache gegeben. Das heute viel beschworene Corporate Design vermittelt sich im Fall der *musica viva* nicht über sperrige Logos und bürokratisch anmutende Institutsmitteilungen, sondern in für kulturelle Veranstaltungen adäquaten Gestaltungen, nämlich ausschließlich über die künstlerische Handschrift eines Grafikers.

Von 1952 bis zu seinem Tod 1963 hatte der Grafiker und Chefbühnenbildner an der Bayerischen Staatsoper Helmut Jürgens die Plakate für die *musica viva* gestaltet. Er wurde von dem Maler Walter Tafelmaier abgelöst. Dieser hatte stets seine Intentionen, die ihn in der Malerei und Grafik beschäftigten, in die Plakate einfließen lassen. Sowohl bei Jürgens als auch bei Tafelmaier ging es darum, die Plakate für die *musica viva* nicht nur als schlichte Ankündigungen zu verstehen oder als Lobpreisungen berühmter Musiker oder Komponisten, sondern mit der öffentlichen Ankündigung die synchronisierte Sprache der Künste sichtbar zu machen.

Als nach Karl Amadeus Hartmann, der die *musica viva*-Konzertreihe des Bayerischen Rundfunks bis zu seinem Tode 1963 leitete, nach Wolfgang Fortner / Ernst Thomas (1964 – 1978) und Jürgen Meyer-Josten (1978 – 1997) der Komponist und damalige Intendant der Oper Leipzig Udo Zimmermann die Künstlerische Leitung der *musica viva* übernahm (1997 – 2011), wurde das kuratorische Team um den Musikwissenschaftler Winrich Hopp und den Komponisten Josef Anton Riedl erweitert. Für die grafische Gestaltung der Werbemedien und Publikationen konnte der Grafiker, Typograf, Verleger, Autor und Sammler Günter Karl Bose gewonnen werden, der auch die Visualität der Konzertreihe prägt, seit Winrich Hopp 2011 die Künstlerische Leitung der *musica viva* übernommen hat.

So unterschiedlich die Grafiker auch sein mögen, es eint sie ein freier Umgang mit der Aufgabe und ihre jeweils höchst individuellen Lösungen. Die Namen Jürgens und Tafelmaier sind untrennbar mit der *musica viva* verbunden und umgekehrt. Das gilt inzwischen längst auch für Günter Karl Bose. In Berlin hatte er bereits für das Literaturhaus mit Plakaten und Prospekten geworben, die durch ihre Eleganz und den ungewöhnlichen Umgang mit Typografie auffielen. Hier knüpfte er auch in seinen Arbeiten für die *musica viva* an. Sie bestechen durch die eigene Rhythmik der bildnerischen Elemente, ihre farbigen Akkorde, das Spiel mit Kontrasten und die kräftig gesetzten Zäsuren und schrillen Töne, die weiten Klangräume, die sich im Spannungsfeld zwischen weißer und bedruckter Fläche aufbauen.

Für die *musica viva* findet Günter Karl Bose, anders als seine Vorgänger, in jedem Jahrgang besondere Gestaltungsansätze. Er nutzt die Mittel Schrift und Bild, Zeichen und Schrift, lässt Ziffern und Buchstaben zum Zeichen werden, kombiniert Zeichnung mit Fotografie und akzentuiert bestimmte Elemente jeweils neu und anders. In den ersten zwei Jahren warb er mit ausschließlich im Querformat entstandenen Plakaten für die Veranstaltungen. Klare Typografie ist darauf mit bald scharfen, bald weniger scharfen fotografischen Bildern kombiniert. Gesichter, Details technischer Geräte, Ausschnitte naturwissenschaftlicher Fotografien, Aufnahmen von Himmelskörpern künden von den Geräuschen der Straße, ja des Alls, deren Pendelschlag am Gerüst quer gezogener, vage an Notenzeilen erinnernder Linien gemessen wird. Meist fett und weithin sichtbar dominiert das jeweilige Veranstaltungsdatum, das sich oft wie ein Paukenschlag im grafischen Orchester Gehör verschafft. Es bildet zugleich das Gegengewicht zu den, das Querformat unterstützenden Linien, ein Prinzip, das der Grafiker zunächst im Sinne der Wiedererkennung die ersten beiden Jahre beibehielt. Seine unverkennbare Eigenart hat die Tradition des Genres Konzertplakat um neue gestalterische Möglichkeiten bereichert.

Schaut man in die Geschichte der Konzertwerbung, findet man eine erstaunliche Bandbreite grafischer Übersetzungen und Deutungen zum Thema Musik. In den 1960er und 1970er Jahren dominierten in Plakaten, die für Konzerte von verschiedensten Rundfunkanstalten warben, oft bewegte geometrische Formen in wiederholten rhythmischen Ordnungen als Gegengewicht zu oft sehr textlastigen Informationen. Namen wie Reinhart Braun, Hans Förtsch und Sigrid von Baumgarten oder Jürgen Spohn, Hans Michel und Günther Kieser stehen hierfür. Letzterer fand seine eigenwillige Sprache dann vor allem in Plakaten, die für Jazz und Popmusik warben. Sie gelten inzwischen als wahre Klassiker, die bis heute Maßstäbe gesetzt haben. Ankündigungen klassischer Musik stellen Grafiker stets vor die schwierige Aufgabe, lange Stücktitel, bisweilen wenig bekannte Komponisten und einzelne Solisten aufführen zu müssen und die Textmenge mit einer sinnlichen und assoziativen Form zu kombinieren oder sie bereits als Teil dieser zu begreifen, um Aufmerksamkeit zu erregen. Irmgard Horlbeck-Kappler übersetzte

Musik in kalligrafische Formen, die sie rhythmisch zu steigern wusste. Ott + Stein haben die Fläche des Papiers als Klangraum begriffen und Schrift und elementare Formen als rhythmische Einheit verstanden. Für die experimentellen Installationen »Klanguhr Hörgalerie«, die über 10 Jahre in Berlin stattfanden, hatte das Atelier cyan aus Leuchtfarben, Schriftform und grafischen Elementen Klangerlebnisse visualisiert.

Obwohl die erste Plakatserie Günter Karl Boses für die *musica viva* wie ein Probelauf für das Ausloten verschiedenster Ausdrucksmöglichkeiten wirkt, werden hier bereits bestimmte Kompositionsprinzipien und Gestaltungsmittel sichtbar, auf die der Grafiker wiederholt zurückgreift: die Gegenüberstellung technischer und geometrischer Formen, die als Bildzeichen zur Schrift stehen, die Verwendung von ausschnitthaften Fotografien, schließlich die Verwandlung von Schriftzeilen in Bänder, die an die Zeiten der Telegrafie erinnern oder die Liveticker, die uns die neuesten Nachrichten als laufendes Band am Rande eines Fernsehbildes übermitteln, das oft mit den Nachrichten gar nichts zu tun hat. Die Gleichzeitigkeit der Ereignisse und Eindrücke im Alltag nutzt der Grafiker, um uns scheinbar vertraute Bilder anders zu präsentieren und darüber die neue Nachricht vom nächsten Konzertereignis mitzuteilen.

Mit dem Wechsel zum Hochformat in der *musica viva*-Saison 1999/2000 setzte Günter Karl Bose seinen freien Umgang mit den grafischen Mitteln fort und begann, bewusst einzelne Elemente wegzulassen, andere wieder aufzugreifen und in neue Zusammenhänge zu stellen. Zunächst verzichtete er auf das fotografische Bild, um nur mit Typografie zu arbeiten. Das klar lesbare, groß gesetzte Veranstaltungsdatum bleibt das optische Signal, das sich über all die Jahre wie ein verbindendes Element durch die Plakatgestaltungen zieht, doch jedes Mal in anderer Form erscheint. Günter Karl Bose stellt sich der immerwährenden Herausforderung, Sehgewohnheiten aufzubrechen, auch die, die er selbst erzeugt. Es geht um die ständige Herstellung von Aufmerksamkeit durch gleichsam unverbrauchte bildnerische Gestaltungen. Wiedererkennbar bleibt die Art, wie er einmal gefundene Ausdrucksmittel neu zusammensetzt oder mit Formen wie etwa dem Streifenelement umgeht. Es erscheint als Textstreifen, mal als Bildzeile, als Raum gliederndes Gitter, als Gegengewicht zu gewebten und vibrierenden Formen.

Wenngleich Günter Karl Bose nie der Versuchung unterlag, Musik, musikalische Rhythmen in grafische Zeichen und rhythmische Geometrien quasi wörtlich zu übersetzen, verlässt er nun ganz die Anspielung auf visualisierte Musik. Vielmehr bewegt er sich in seiner individuellen Bildsprache, die ihren eigenen Gesetzen folgt. Parallel zur modernen Musik, die traditionelles Tonmaterial mit dem tonalen Klangspektrum der gegenwärtigen Alltagswelt kombiniert oder ersteres ganz zugunsten des letzteren aufgibt, bedient sich Günter Karl Bose der unterschiedlichsten Bildquellen aus dem Alltag als Formmaterial. Er schaut dabei nicht auf die Kunst, sondern auf die über unterschiedliche Medien verbreiteten Bilder, die alltäglich konsumierten Fotografien, Plakate, Inserate, Verpackungen, Tapeten und Ornamente ebenso wie auf die Hinterlassenschaften der zum Massenphänomen angewachsenen Amateurfotografie. Das verbindende Thema zur modernen Musik ist die Wahrnehmung des Alltäglichen. Der Grafiker hebt das Banale und teilweise Triviale ins Erhabene durch Verfremdung. Aus dem Repertoire der Alltagsbilder werden Figuren, Gegenstände, Formen farbig überhöht, grafisch gerastert, aus ihren Kontexten herausgelöst, ohne diese gänzlich zu verleugnen und mit elementaren Formen kombiniert. Immer wieder greift der Grafiker und leidenschaftliche Sammler von Amateurfotografie auf das Foto zurück. Häufig nutzt er Details fotografischer Aufnahmen, die zunächst wie beiläufige Zufallsprodukte anmuten, doch überblendet oder umrahmt von den grafischen Formen, eingebettet in den Rhythmus der Typografie zugleich geheimnisvoll wie assoziativ wirken.

Die Saison 2000/01 eröffnete er mit einem Plakat für »Szenische Konzerte mit Percussionisten«. Es ist mit einem Foto unterlegt, das Scherben einer zerschlagenen Leuchte zeigt, einer Sicherung und Glühlampenfassung. Darüber wird die explosive Sprengkraft musikalischer Darbietungen ahnbar. Doch nicht das Illustrative, sondern das Vorgestellte, das Mögliche und auch Verstörende steht im Mittelpunkt des bildnerischen Kommentars. Mitunter greift Günter Karl Bose bewusst auf Bilder aus modernen Hochglanzmagazinen zurück, sucht er optische Anknüpfungen an vertraute Bilder von Fetischen wie Schuh und Handtasche, nutzt Bilder bekannter Figurenposen quasi als verfremdete Folie des Alltags, um auf die parallel stattfindenden, sich von diesem Alltag zugleich abhebenden wie dazugehörenden *musica viva*-Konzerte aufmerksam zu machen.

Er strebt nie Bildhaftigkeit an. Seine Plakate sind stets dominiert von Bild- und Schriftzeichen, die dem Takt einer eigenen grafischen Choreographie folgen. Für jeweils einen Jahrgang behält er oft bestimmte Elemente im Layout bei, die auf Wiedererkennung zielen. Dann wieder wechseln die Erscheinungsbilder von Kombinationen gezeichneter Formen mit Schrift zu Montagen oder zu rein typografischen Gestaltungen. So wird der Auftakt der Saison 2001/02 mit dem unübersehbaren Datum 26.10.01 beworben. Die Geometrie der Ziffern erinnert an die koreanischer Schriftzeichen und fällt zunächst in ihrer ungewöhnlichen Strenge auf. Dieses Auffallen und Sich-Absetzen vom Alltäglichen durchzieht das ganze grafische Konzept Günter Karl Boses. Das ungewöhnliche Datum wird zur gestalterischen Konstante der Saison 2001/02. Im letzten Plakat ist es groß in die Fläche gesetzt, gleichsam eingeschmolzen, leicht zurücktretend hinter der bewusst erzielten Unschärfe des Farbverlaufs, der hier bereits auf die Gestaltung für die nächste Saison verweist, ohne sie vorweg zu nehmen. Oft jedoch macht der Grafiker nicht etwa da weiter, wo die Werbung für die letzte Saison geendet hatte, sondern wählt einen neuen wirkungsvollen Auftritt, sich der Tatsache bewusst, dass die letzten Plakate über die Sommerpause hinweg bei vielen längst in Vergessenheit geraten sind. Er setzt Einfachheit und Leere in die Fülle des Alltags oder überrascht mit bewusst gewählter Formfülle.

Günter Karl Bose ist ein genauer Beobachter und Kenner der öffentlichen Bildkommunikation. Er analysiert Bildsprachen der massenhaft verbreiteten Bilder in der Werbung wie in den unterschiedlichsten Medien und baut daraus eine Gegenstrategie auf. Die reagiert auch kurzfristig. Der Grafiker schaut, was im Stadtraum passiert, um seine Stimme dem Gleichklang im Chor der Werbebilder zu widersetzen. Er nimmt in Kauf, nicht sofort entschlüsselt zu werden, sondern provoziert den zweiten und dritten Blick, veranlasst den Beschauer, über die sinnliche Erfahrung der Form zur Information zu kommen. Er arbeitet mit Irritation. Wenngleich immer wieder Bildelemente in den Folgejahren Verwendung finden, überwiegt die gestaltende Kraft der Typografie. Souverän setzt der Grafiker hier groß gegen klein, fett gegen schmal, baut er Schriftbänder und -türme auf, grafische Gitterwerke auf Stoß gesetzter Schrifttypen, lässt Lettern als Zeichen einer rhythmischen Komposition erscheinen, die ihre Dynamik aus dem zuweilen extrem ausgereizten Wechsel von gedruckter Form und den Zwischenräumen entwickelt, die mal eng, mal weit sind, sich aus der Umschließung lösen und selbst Form bilden. Nicht immer macht es der Grafiker dem Betrachter leicht: Er soll nicht schnell wahrnehmen und ebenso schnell vergessen, sondern er soll gefesselt werden, durch eine Form, eine Figur, durch Farbe, und die von Bewegung und Rhythmus ausgelöste Emotionalität ebenso wie von der Magie des Vertrauten, das stets unvertraut erscheint. Hier wieder treffen sich die Intentionen des Grafikers mit denen gegenwärtigen Musikschaffens.

Dass der Bayerische Rundfunk und der Künstlerische Leiter der *musica viva* noch immer auf das oft tot gesagte Medium Plakat vertrauen, spricht für Weitsicht und ein Kulturverständnis, das dem gedruckten Papier noch immer die Bedeutung einräumt, die es verdient. Seit dem Siegeszug der digitalen Medien wird der Unkenruf vom Tod eines Mediums laut, obwohl sich herausgestellt hat, dass es nichts Vergleichbares gibt. Das Plakat zieht seine besondere Wirkung aus der Fläche, die sich uns unvermittelt als Visitenkarte eines Auftraggebers, Grafikers, einer Institution und Stadt entgegenstellt und wesentlich das Niveau der visuellen Kultur unseres Alltags bestimmt. Darin liegt eine hohe Verantwortung, und man kann die *musica viva* des Bayerischen Rundfunks beglückwünschen, dieser in jeder Hinsicht gerecht zu werden.

Anita Kühnel:

The Courage to Pursue New Formulations.
Günter Karl Bose's works for *musica viva*

The Swiss Armin Hofmann referred to the graphic designer's sphere of activity as a distinct world of sound resulting from the combination of images and writing. As Hofmann wrote, "The harmonious combination of two different systems necessarily presupposes a deepening of the artistic sensibility as well as the courage to pursue new avenues of thought and formulations."

I encountered my first *musica viva* poster on an advertising pillar near a train station when I was travelling from Berlin to Munich in 2008. Its unusual black shapes, seemingly a bit cryptic at first glance, cast a spell on me as they triumphed like exclamation marks over the wide white space of the paper on which they were printed. With this enchanting welcome, I was not only greeted by the cultural metropolis of Munich and Bayerischer Rundfunk—the Bavarian radio broadcaster and presenter of an important concert series of modern and avant-garde music— but also by the idiosyncratic voice of a graphic artist for whom Armin Hofmann's words could serve as a guide.

For now 20 years, Günter Karl Bose has been the graphic artist behind the posters, program booklets and postcards for the ambitious *musica viva* concert series. Ever dedicated to the musical creations of the present, *musica viva* has been with us for more than 70 years. An internationally acclaimed institution, the series remains committed to the living tradition of promoting contemporary music and true to the motto postulated by its founder: "Music is a language of the present". In 1945, with the support of the administration of the American military, Karl Amadeus Hartmann, composer and then newly appointed dramaturge of the Bayerische Staatstheater (Bavarian State Theaters), began regular concerts of contemporary music with the Bayerisches Staatsorchester (Bavarian State Orchestra). The name 'musica viva' was given to the series in July of 1947. From 1948 onwards, the concerts took place in conjunction with Radio München, which would later become Bayerischer Rundfunk. When the Symphonieorchester des Bayerischen Rundfunks (Bavarian Radio Symphony Orchestra) was founded in 1949, Bayerischer Rundfunk integrated Karl Amadeus Hartmann's *musica viva* concert series, whereupon the orchestra became its committed and most significant partner. Since then, the orchestra has premiered countless compositions commissioned and produced by Bayerischer Rundfunk's *musica viva*, performances that are broadcast from the concert hall to the greater public as part of the BR-Klassik radio program. It is especially important that the liveliness of the musical language of the present be constantly reflected in visually inviting promotional media. Just as *musica viva* has always made its stage available to a wide variety of musical temperaments, since its inception it has also provided a free space for the graphic artists engaged in the production of its publications to develop a visual language. In using this language to address the public, *musica viva* does not communicate via the cumbersome logos and bureaucracy-tinged institutional messages of today's much-vaunted corporate design. Instead it relies exclusively on the creative handiwork of the graphic artist to convey its message in a manner more appropriate for cultural events.

From 1952 until his death in 1963, graphic artist and chief set designer for the Bayerische Staatsoper (Bavarian State Opera) Helmut Jürgens designed the concert posters for *musica viva*. After his death, he was replaced by the painter Walter Tafelmaier, whose posters often displayed the influence of themes that occupied him in painting and graphic arts. Both Jürgens and Tafelmaier understood the *musica viva* posters to be more than mere advertisement or a celebration of famous musicians or composers. For these graphic artists, the posters were an opportunity to make publicly visible the synchronized language of the arts.

After Karl Amadeus Hartmann, who led Bayerischer Rundfunk's *musica viva* until his death in 1963, and the subsequent directorships of Wolfgang Fortner/Ernst Thomas (1964 – 1978) and Jürgen Meyer-Josten (1978 – 1997), composer Udo Zimmermann, director of the Oper Leipzig (Leipzig Opera) at the time, assumed artistic leadership from 1997 to 2011. During his term, he expanded the curatorial staff to include musicologist Winrich Hopp and composer Josef Anton Riedl. Graphic designer, typographer, publisher, author and collector Günter Karl Bose was persuaded to handle the graphic design of promotional media and publications. Since Winrich Hopp took over the artistic directorship of *musica viva* in 2011, Bose's visual artistry has come to characterize the overall aesthetic of the concert series.

As different as graphic designers may be from one another, they are alike in their free approach to a task and unified by the high degree of individuality that distinguishes each artist's solution. The names Jürgens and Tafelmaier are inextricably linked to *musica viva* and vice versa, and this has long been true of the name Günter Karl Bose as well. Before joining *musica viva*, Bose had previously created promotional posters and leaflets for Berlin's Literaturhaus, outstanding for their elegance and unusual typography. He built on this work for his *musica viva* designs, which feature their own particular rhythm of pictorial elements, colorful chords, play of contrasts, vigorously placed caesuras, shrill tones, and the vast sound environments that build up in the tension between printed regions and white space.

Unlike his predecessors, Bose finds unique designs for each succeeding year. His means are varied: text combined with images; symbols combined with text; numerals and letters blended to form symbols. He melds illustration with photography, accentuating his compositions in unprecedented ways. In his first two years of *musica viva* work, the event posters were rendered exclusively in landscape format. In these Bose combines clearly defined typography with photographic images, some in sharp focus while others are somewhat blurred. The compositions feature faces, details of technical equipment and cutouts from natural-science photographs. Photographs of celestial bodies tell of the noise of the street—or even that of the universe, whose pendulum swing is measured on a grid of horizontal lines vaguely similar to a music staff. Usually in bold print and visible from afar, the date of the featured event typically dominates the poster. It makes itself heard like the beat of a drum in the midst of a graphic orchestra. At the same time, the date forms a counterweight to the lines supporting the oblong format, a design feature the artist maintained for the first two years to bolster viewer recognition. Bose's unmistakable style enriched the tradition of the concert poster genre by introducing new possibilities for creativity.

In looking at the history of concert advertising, one finds an astonishing range of graphic translations and interpretations of music. Very popular in promotional concert posters published by an array of radio stations in the 1960s and 1970s were the animated geometric forms portrayed in repeated, rhythmic patterns that balanced messages heavily reliant on text. Examples of this technique are found in the work of artists such as Reinhart Braun, Hans Förtsch, Sigrid von Baumgarten, Jürgen Spohn, Hans Michel and Günther Kieser. The latter found his unique manner of expression particularly in posters promoting jazz and pop music. These posters are considered true classics that set standards even today. Advertisements for classical music always present graphic artists with the challenge of incorporating long composition titles and the names of sometimes little-known composers and soloists. To draw the eye, these must be combined with text in a sensual and associative design or even rendered as a unified part of that design. Irmgard Horlbeck-Kappler knew how to translate music into calligraphic configurations that she intensified rhythmically. Ott + Stein saw the paper surface as a sort of sound space and understood the rhythmic unity of text and elementary shapes. In its more than ten-year run of experimental Klanguhr Hörgalerie installations in Berlin, Atelier Cyan visualized sound with luminous colors, text and graphics.

Although Bose's first poster series for *musica viva* seems like an exploration of the most diverse range of possibilities of expression, certain principles and means of compositional design were already visible to which the artist would later return repeatedly. We see the contrast of technical and geometric forms used as visual symbols to complement the text, the use of fragments of photographs and, finally, the transformation of lines of text into bands reminiscent of the era of telegraph ticker tape or even today's news ticker streaming along the bottom of an often totally unrelated TV image. Bose takes advantage of this everyday conjunction of events and impressions to present seemingly familiar images to us in an unexpected way as a means to deliver the message of an upcoming concert.

With the switch to portrait format for the 1999 – 2000 *musica viva* season, Bose continued his liberal approach in his use of graphic media. At this stage, he began the deliberate omission of some compositional elements while taking up previously used ones once more, albeit in wholly new contexts. While he did away with photographic images to work exclusively with typography, the clearly legible and large-scale event date remained the optical signal. This feature was a unifying element in the poster designs year after year despite changes in style and appearance. Bose takes on the ever-present challenge of breaking habits of observation—even those he himself has created. A key element here is sustaining viewer attention through largely uncommon visual constructs. What remains recognizably characteristic throughout his work is his recombination of found means of expression in fresh ways as well as the use of concepts such as linear, strip-like forms. This theme may appear as a ribbon of text or the lines of a monitor screen, as a lattice bridging space or a counterweight to interwoven or vibrating shapes.

Although Bose never succumbed to the temptation of translating music or musical rhythm literally, so to speak, into graphic and rhythmic geometries, he now wholly departs from any allusion to visualized music, moving instead in a pictorial language of his own making that follows its own rules. Contemporary music combines traditional material with the tonal spectrum of the modern, everyday world (when not abandoning the former entirely for the sake of the latter). Similarly, Bose taps the most diverse sources of everyday images for his visual material. Rather than art, he is drawn to the images spread across all sorts of media. Of interest to him is our daily diet of photographic images, posters, advertisements, packaging, wallpaper patterns and ornamentation as well as the endless troves of amateur photography—the legacy of its phenomenal mass popularity. What unites photography to contemporary music is the perception of the everyday. Through alienation, Bose elevates the banal and the trivial to the sublime. Taken from the repertoire of everyday life, his compositions contain images, figures, objects and shapes that are exaggeratedly colored, graphically rasterized, extracted from context (without completely denying that context) and combined with elementary forms. Bose, both graphic artist and passionate collector of amateur photography, returns to the photographic image perennially in his work. He often uses details of photographs that at first glance appear to be incidental products of chance. Yet blended with or framed by graphic elements, embedded in the rhythm of typography, these have an effect that is both mysterious and associative.

The 2000 – 2001 *musica viva* season was announced with a poster promoting a program entitled "Scenic Percussion Performances". The composition contains a photo of the shards of a shattered lamp, a fuse and lightbulb socket. Here the explosive power of musical performances is inferred by the viewer. It is not the illustrative, but rather the imagined, the possible and the disturbing that are the focus of this pictorial commentary. Sometimes Bose picks up images from today's glossy magazines. He looks for visual connections to familiar images of fetishes such as shoes and handbags. He makes use of pictures of figures in well-known poses to form something like an alienated background of the everyday. Ultimately, these serve to draw attention to *musica viva* concerts, which occur parallel to everyday life, simultaneously belonging and standing out in contrast to it.

He never aspires to the picturesque. His posters are always dominated by images and text that follow the tact of their own graphic choreography. For each year's concert season, he typically maintains certain compositional elements to assure recognition on the part of the viewer, but the look of the posters changes from combinations of illustrations and text to montages or purely typographic designs. Exemplary of this is the 2001 – 2002 season, whose opening-night poster boldly trumpeted the event date. Here the geometry of the numerals, suggestive of Korean characters, is immediately striking for its uncommon severity. Conspicuousness and contrast to everyday life are themes that run through Bose's style as a graphic artist. The unusual presentation of the concert date in his posters became the design constant in 2001 – 2002. In the final poster of that season, the date is assertively large, yet it also appears to melt, as it were, slightly receding behind the intentionally blurred gradient—here already a reference to next season's design without anticipating it. Often, however, Bose does not merely continue where the promotional campaign of the last season left off. Instead, he will choose a striking new look altogether, aware of the fact that the previous season's poster designs have been forgotten by many in the interval of the summer break. His works may insert simplicity and emptiness into the fullness of everyday life or surprise with an abundance of carefully selected imagery.

Günter Karl Bose is a discerning observer and connoisseur of the communication of images in public spaces. He analyzes the pictorial languages of mass-distributed images—from advertising as well as all sorts of other media—to construct a counter-strategy capable of quick response. This artist observes what is happening in the urban environment only to set his own voice in opposition to the unified chorus of advertising images. He does not expect his work to be deciphered immediately, but relies on the provocation of a second and third glance, inducing the viewer to discover the information through a sensory experience of the images and forms. Irritation of the viewer is used as a tool. Even though particular visual elements recur over the years, the creative power of typography ultimately reigns supreme in Bose's graphic compositions. Typefaces are characteristically large rather than small and bold print takes precedence over standard. Text is unfurled in bands, used to build towers, and compressed fonts form the foundations of graphic lattices. Letters appear as symbols in a rhythmic composition whose dynamics develop out of the at times extremely intense interchange between printed forms and intervening spaces. These spaces, narrow or wide, detach themselves from their surroundings and become forms unto themselves. As a graphic designer, Bose does not always make it easy for the viewer, who is supposed to neither perceive nor forget quickly. The viewer is meant to be captivated by form, figure, color, the movement and rhythm of triggered emotion as well as the magic of the familiar consistently portrayed as its opposite. Here again the intentions of the graphic artist converge with those of the creation of contemporary music.

That Bayerischer Rundfunk and the artistic directorship of *musica viva* still rely on the oft-declared dead medium of the printed, paper poster speaks of a foresight and cultural understanding that continues to grant the poster the recognition it deserves. Since the triumph of digital media, loudly prophesizing the doom of the poster medium has been common—despite the fact that it has been shown to have no equal. The unique effect of the poster comes from its surface, abruptly confronting us as it does like a business card, be it that of a client, graphic artist, institution or city. The poster largely determines the degree of visual culture of our everyday life. This is a great responsibility, and one can congratulate Bayerischer Rundfunk's *musica viva* on fulfilling it in every respect.

Paul Klee, der wie Lyonel Feininger lange Zeit geschwankt hatte, ob er nicht selbst Musiker werden sollte, sprach gern und betont von »formaler Symphonik« oder von der »bildnerischen Polyphonie.« Er verstand darunter die selbständige Entfaltung und freie Führung jedes einzelnen bildnerischen Elements, ihre Zusammenordnung zu einzelnen Formgruppen, die Aufgliederung und den Wiederaufbau zum Ganzen auf mehreren Seiten zugleich, die Herstellung des Zusammenklangs durch Ausgleich der bildnerischen Abläufe und Bewegungen. [...] Dabei war alles darauf angelegt, nicht etwa Musik zu kopieren, sondern jedes bildnerische oder musikalische Element so zu definieren, daß die identischen Möglichkeiten sichtbar wurden. [...] Es geht nicht darum, »Musik zu malen«, sondern Erkenntnisse, die an einem Ort gewonnen wurden, für einen anderen Ort nutzbar zu machen. [...] Durch den Kontakt mit der Musik und ihren Verfahren gelang es, das Instrument Malerei subtiler zu machen, sprachfähiger für die Erfahrungen und Erregungen des modernen Geistes, der sich einer Welt gegenüberbefand, die sich zunehmend in Schwingungen, proportionale Gefüge, bewegte Gleichgewichtigkeiten und Zahlengefüge – kurz, ins Abstrakte verschob. Die Analogie zur Musik und zu ihren gegenstandsfreien Ordnungen war da gewiß sehr hilfreich

Werner Haftmann: Musik und moderne Malerei [1959]

Paul Klee, who, like Lyonel Feininger, long vacillated over whether he himself should become a musician, spoke enthusiastically and emphatically of the "formal symphonic" or the "pictorial polyphony". He understood those terms to mean the independent development and unfettered execution of each individual pictorial element, their distribution into individual form groups, the classification and reconstruction of the whole from multiple perspectives simultaneously, and the creation of harmony through the balancing of pictorial processes and movements. [...] In doing so, the point was not at all to copy music, but rather to define each pictorial or musical element so that identical possibilities became visible. [...] The idea is not to "paint music", but rather to take realizations gained in one place and make them useful in another. [...] Through contact with music and its process, it became possible to make the instrument of painting more subtle, more capable of expressing the experiences and excitement of a modern mind that found itself facing a world increasingly sliding into oscillation, proportional structures, fluctuating balances, and number configurations; simply put, into the abstract. The analogy to music and its non-representational systems was certainly very helpful, but it was not the matter at hand. The matter at hand was to reach the

Werner Haftmann: Musik und moderne Malerei [1959]

Appendix

Textnachweis | text reference

Max Bense: *Plakatwelt* in ders: *Plakatwelt. Vier Essays*. Stuttgart 1952 [DVA Stuttgart], S. 9 – 22.

Werner Haftmann: *Musik und moderne Malerei* in K. H. Ruppel [Ed.]: *Musica Viva*. München 1959 [Nymphenburger Verlagshandlung], S. 173 – 195.

Literatur | bibliography

musica viva-*Konzertreihe | concert series*

K.H. Ruppel [Ed.]: *Musica Viva*. München 1959 [Nymphenburger Verlagshandlung].

Renata Wagner [Ed.]: *Karl Amadeus Hartmann und die Musica Viva*. München 1980 [Piper Verlag].

Renate Ulm [Ed.]: *Eine Sprache der Gegenwart: musica viva 1945 –1995*. Mainz 1995 [Schott].

Winrich Hopp: *Musica Viva. Über die Vergangenheit der bedeutenden Münchner Veranstaltungsreihe und wie sie sich selbst neu kreiert*. In: *Das Orchester*. 3. 2002, S. 17–24.

musica viva-*Plakate | posters*

IDEA 292, Tokyo 2002.

area. 100 graphic designers 10 curators. New York 2003 [Phaidon Press].

Summit. Die besten Plakate am Ende des 20. Jahrhunderts. [PAN Kunstforum Niederrhein]. Emmerich 2003.

PAGE 06.2004, S. 11.

Günter Karl Bose: *Plakate + andere Drucksachen für musica viva '97 bis '05*. München 2005 [Bayerischer Rundfunk].

Nancy Skolos, Thomas Wedell [Ed.]: *Type, Image, Message*. Gloucester, Massachusetts 2006 [Rockport Publishers].

Robert Klanten, Mika Mischler, Boris Brummjak: *Serialize, Faces and Variety in Graphic Design*. Berlin 2006 [= Die Gestalten Verlag].

Melchior Imboden [Ed.]: *Designer Portraits*. Berlin/Sulgen 2007 [Hesign Publishing/ Niggli Verlag].

Ben Bos, Elly Bos [Ed.]: *AGI. Graphic Design since 1950*. London, New York 2007 [Thames & Hudson].

Cees de Jong, Stephanie Burger, Jorre Both: *New Poster Art*. London / New York 2008 [Thames & Hudson].

6+6. Deutsche und Taiwanesische Plakate in Taipeh. Berlin/Hangzhou 2009 [Hesign Publishing].

Larissa Kowal-Wolk: *Unerhörte Bilder*. In: *BR Klassik. Musikmagazin des Bayerischen Rundfunks* 1. 2009, S. 12-13.

De Sein. German Graphic Design from Postwar to Present. [InnoCentre Hong Kong] Berlin, Hangzhou 2011 [Hesign Publishing].

Alliance Graphique Internationale. German Members. Deutsche Mitglieder. 1954–2011. Berlin 2011 [Hesign Publishing].

Cees de Jong, Alston Purvis, Martijn F. Le Coultre: *The Poster. 1000 Posters from Toulouse-Lautrec to Sagmeister*. New York 2011 [Abrams].

Anita Kühnel [Ed.]: *Welt aus Schrift. Das 20. Jahrhundert in Europa und den USA*. [Kunstbibliothek- Staatliche Museen zu Berlin]. Köln 2011 [Verlag der Buchhandlung Walther König].

Boris Brummjak: *100 Schwarz-Weiss-Plakate. Aus der Sammlung Boris Brummjak*. Luzern 2013 [Kunsthalle Luzern].

Anita Kühnel [Ed.]: *Schrift. Bild. Zeichen. Werbegrafik in Deutschland 1945–2015*. [Kunstbibliothek- Staatliche Museen zu Berlin]. Dortmund 2016 [Verlag Kettler].

Internet | websites

http://www.br-musica-viva.de
http://www.lmn-berlin.com
http://a-g-i.org/members

Ausstellungen | exhibitions

2003
Summit. Die besten Plakate am Ende des 20. Jahrhunderts. PAN Kunstforum Niederrhein.

2004
Tehran International Poster Biennial. Tehran.

2005
German AGI Graphic Design: Perfect Form. Ginza Graphic Gallery Tokyo.

Festival International de l'Affiche et des Arts Graphique de Chaumont (France).

Plakate und andere Drucksachen für musica viva. Bayerischer Rundfunk München.

2009
6+6. Deutsche und Taiwanesische Plakate in Taipeh. National Chiang Kai-shek Memorial Hall, Taipeh, Taiwan.

2011
German Graphic Design from Postwar to Present. InnoCentre, Hong Kong.

Welt aus Schrift. Das 20. Jahrhundert in Europa und den USA. Kunstbibliothek – Staatliche Museen zu Berlin.

Sammlungen | collections

Kunstbibliothek
Staatliche Museen zu Berlin

Folkwang Museum Essen

Museum für Kunst und Gewerbe
Hamburg

Museum für Angewandte Kunst
Frankfurt am Main

Deutsches Buch- und Schriftmuseum
der Deutschen Nationalbibliothek Leipzig

Bibliothèque Nationale Paris

Museum für Gestaltung Zürich

Preise | awards

100 BESTE PLAKATE

1997.98 02	1997.98 04
1998.99 04	1998.99 07
2000.01 01	2000.01 07
2002.03 01	2002.03 04
2002.03 05	2003.04 02
2005.06 03	2005.06 09
2006.07 07	2006.07 08
2007.08 03	2010.11 02
2015.16 05	

Kulturplakat des Monats München

2000.01 06	2002.03 01
2002.03 05	2003.04 02

Teheran International Poster Biennial

2002.03 04

Festival International de Chaumont

2002.03 04	2004.05 02

Biografien | biographies

Dr. ANITA KÜHNEL ist Kunsthistorikerin. Von 1978 bis 1992 war sie wissenschaftliche Mitarbeiterin am Kupferstichkabinett der Staatlichen Museen zu Berlin, von 1992 bis 2016 Leiterin der Sammlung Grafikdesign der Kunstbibliothek der Staatlichen Museen zu Berlin. Veröffentlichungen zur Grafik und zum Grafikdesign des 19. und 20. Jahrhunderts.

Dr. ANITA KÜHNEL is an art historian. She was a research assistant at the Kupferstichkabinett der Staatlichen Museen zu Berlin from 1978 to 1992, and from 1992 to 2016, she was the director of the graphic-design collection at the Kunstbibliothek der Staatlichen Museen zu Berlin. She has published works on graphic arts and design of the 19th and 20th centuries.

GÜNTER KARL BOSE [*1951] ist Gestalter, Lehrer und Sammler. Er studierte Germanistik und Politikwissenschaft an der Universität Freiburg. Von 1980 bis 1995 war er Verleger in Berlin [Brinkmann & Bose]. Seit 1993 ist er Professor für Typografie an der Hochschule für Grafik und Buchkunst in Leipzig und leitet dort das Institut für Buchkunst. Er hat zahlreiche Bücher zur Kultur- und Mediengeschichte veröffentlicht, zuletzt *Stardust. Ein Kapitel aus der Geschichte des Gesichts* [2015] und *Bookish! Ein Rückblick* [2017].

GÜNTER KARL BOSE [*1951] is a designer, teacher and collector. He studied German philology and political science at the University of Freiburg. From 1980 to 1995 he worked as an editor in Berlin [Brinkmann & Bose]. Since 1993, he has been a Professor of Typography at the Hochschule für Grafik und Buchkunst in Leipzig [Academy of Fine Arts], where he is also head of the Institut für Buchkunst [Institute of Book Arts]. He has published numerous books on the history of culture and media, his latest *Stardust. Ein Kapitel aus der Geschichte des Gesichts* [2015] and *Bookish! Ein Rückblick* [2017].

Impressum | imprint

Günter Karl Bose
for musica viva / für musica viva
Posters / Plakate 1997 – 2017

Gestaltung | graphic design:
Günter Karl Bose

Redaktion | editing:
Lu Antonia Bose

Bildbearbeitung | lithography:
Uwe Langner

Übersetzung | translation:
Warren La Guzza

Herstellung | production:
Aumüller Regensburg

Erschienen bei | published by
Spector Books
Harkortstraße 10
04107 Leipzig
www.spectorbooks.com

Distribution
Germany, Austria: GVA, Gemeinsame Verlagsauslieferung Göttingen GmbH & Co. KG,
www.gva-verlage.de
Switzerland: AVA Verlagsauslieferung AG,
www.ava.ch
France, Belgium: Interart Paris, www.interart.fr
UK: Central Books Ltd, www.centralbooks.com
USA, Canada, Central and South America, Africa, Asia: ARTBOOK/ D.A.P., www.artbook.com
South Korea: The Book Society,
www.thebooksociety.org
Australia, New Zealand: Perimeter Distribution,
www.perimeterdistribution.com

© 2017 Günter Karl Bose
Spector Books, Leipzig

1. Auflage | first edition
Printed in Germany

ISBN 978-3-95905-141-5

1

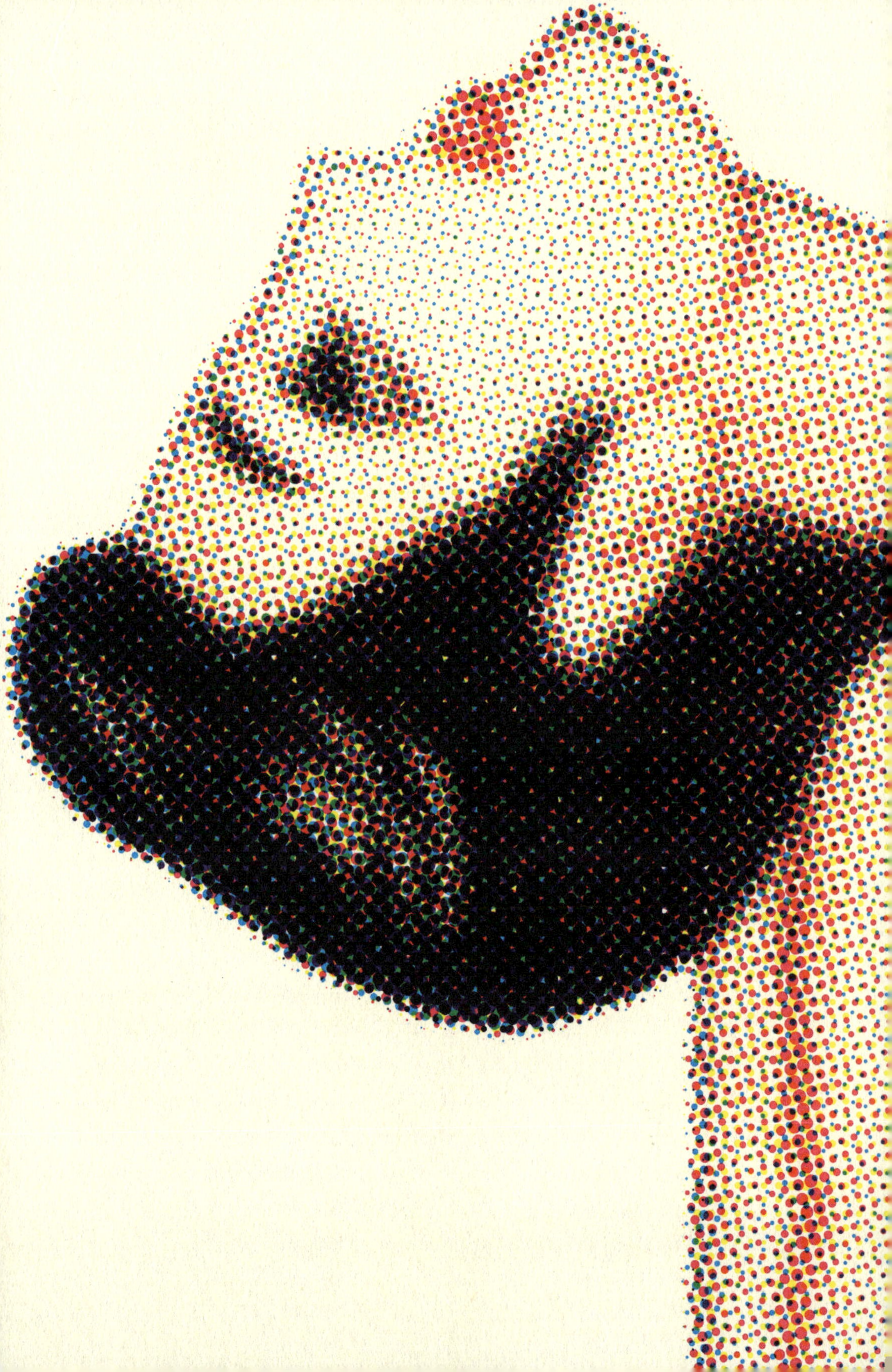

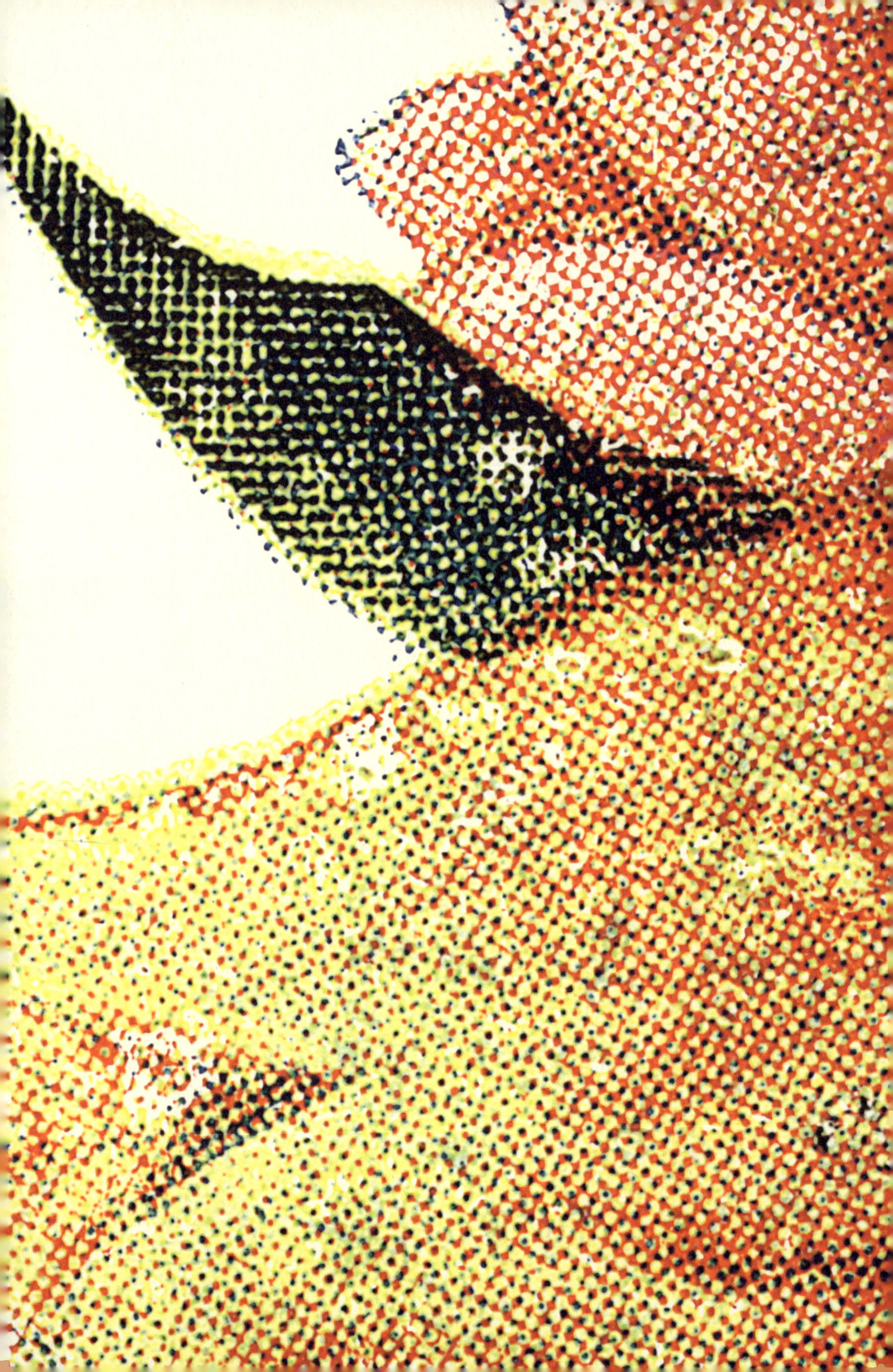